IL DIVO

Our Music, Our Journey, Our Words

IL DIVO

Our Music, Our Journey, Our Words

headline

First published in 2007 by
HEADLINE PUBLISHING GROUP

First published in paperback in 2008 by
HEADLINE PUBLISHING GROUP

1

Cataloguing in Publication Data is available from the British Library

ISBN 978 0 7553 1658 8

Designed by Perfect Bound Ltd
Printed and bound in Italy by
Canale and C.S.p.A

Headline's policy is to use papers that are natural, renewable and recyclable products and made from wood grown in sustainable forests. The logging and manufacturing processes are expected to conform to the environmental regulations of the country of origin.

HEADLINE PUBLISHING GROUP
A division of Hachette Livre UK Ltd
338 Euston Road
London NW1 3BH

Special thanks to:
Emma Tait, Bernard Dive, Emily Furniss and everyone else at Headline Publishing Group, Dan Newman at Perfect Bound Ltd, Borra Garson at Deborah McKenna Ltd, Barbara Nash, Danny Emmett, Dave Shack at SONY BMG, Laurence Boakes at SYCO Music, Howard Wilmot, Cat Ross at Warwick Worldwide and the Moderators.

Photograph Credits:
Bernardo Doral: 2/3, 7, 8, 18, 22, 32, 43, 48, 51, 56/57, 63, 67, 70, 75, 76, 80/81, 89, 97, 106, 114/115, 119, 128, 131, 136/137, 139, 149, 175, 176, 184/185, 190/191.
Dean Hammer: 5, 15, 24, 30/31, 36/37, 38, 64, 72, 86, 100/101, 109, 116, 122, 143, 155, 166, 171, 172, 178, 179.
Kevin Mazur: 11, 29, 52, 53, 94, 113, 132, 168.
Andrew Wong: 13, 140.
Christopher Wahl: 17, 41, 46/47, 54, 60, 78/79, 98, 105, 120, 124/125, 146, 150, 164/165, 181.
Neil Kirk: 21, 68/69, 82, 84, 90/91, 111, 134/135, 153, 156/157, 159.
Juan Sánchez Espejo HOLA!: 26/27.
Larry Bussaca: 35.
Michel Comte: 59, 102, 144, 187.
New Liberty Productions: 93.
Yuka Yamaji: 127.
Walter Chin: 162, 182.
Kambouris/Getty Images: 189.

www.headline.co.uk
www.hachettelivre.co.uk
www.ildivo.com

Contents

Preface

Il Divo

Being in Il Divo has been a rollercoaster ride, an amazing and extraordinary journey. It's incredible to look back to when this all began and realize what we have achieved. Each time the lights are switched on and our performances begin, we have just one thing in mind: to give our fans 110 per cent. There is nothing more rewarding than seeing our fans enjoy our music and this book has been written for them…

We see it as a unique opportunity to share the stories of our lives and the passions that have got us here today. We were determined to tell the truth about ourselves, our relationships and the events in our lives in our own words. Each of us has written about our highs and lows, our disappointments and joys. We have talked about topics that have never been published before and, where necessary, we've tried to set the record straight.

We hope the book will answer all the questions that have ever been put to us and give our fans a unique and real insight into our lives; a journey so many of them share with their ongoing support.

Peter Rudge

Il Divo is Italian for divine performer and there could be no better name for the four charismatic young men who, for nearly three years, have been on a meteoric journey to international fame and stardom.

I came into Il Divo's life just as their first album was to be launched in the UK. The first track I ever heard was 'Unbreak My Heart', and although by then I had been in the music business for nearly forty years, I realized I was hearing something totally original and unique. Even so, I don't think I fully appreciated at that moment just how successful they would become.

What has happened since has been simply staggering. As the record industry deals with declining CD sales, Il Divo have gone from strength to strength, bucking that trend in countries around the world. Their sound achieves something that is so difficult: it creates a universal appeal by setting aside cultural differences and speaking to music lovers of all ages. We talk about music fulfilling a need in our lives – how it reminds us of good, bad, happy and sad times – and there is no doubt that Il Divo has met this need in millions of fans. A totally unique quartet, they have an extraordinary ability to tap into what touches people's hearts.

The concept of Il Divo was masterminded by Simon Cowell and launched in the UK in November 2004, after a two-year talent search of international opera houses and concert halls. Chosen from thousands of hopefuls, the partnering of Carlos, David, Sébastien and Urs once again confirmed Simon's remarkable talent for spotting gifted singers and his instinct for what people want to hear. With Il Divo he brought an entirely new sound to the world of popular music, a sound that brought the passion and virtuosity of the singers' operatic technique and training to the interpretation of popular romantic songs.

Il Divo is comprised of four incredibly strong and talented individuals. There is no lead singer. They each approach their membership of Il Divo from a slightly different angle and they are very respectful of each other's roles. They don't only have musical talent, they have talent as human beings. They are all very likeable and are able to project that likeability, which is so important. They are gracious and mindful of their relative inexperience of the world they now inhabit and I have always found them appreciative of the experience that we as a management team have to offer.

Carlos sees life in black and white; there's no shade in between. He shoots from the hip and says what he thinks. He believes he knows in an instant what is right for Il Divo, and his intuition usually proves remarkably accurate. He drives everybody crazy when he is at his most obsessive – there is always a moment with Carlos when we know that no logic or further intellectual explanation will satisfy him! Yet we forgive him because of his passion for and dedication to Il Divo.

David can be very hard to read at times. He applies a scientific approach to the business and feels he understands exactly why Il Divo is successful and what it is they need to do to continue to get it right. He is the one who questions the creative process the most – for instance, the choice of songs for the live shows, the packaging of the albums, and so on. David is very intelligent, well-read and analytical and so he looks for precise solutions in an imprecise world. His role in the group is to push the boat out further each time. I really enjoy his company and we debate and laugh a lot together.

Sébastien is the most sensitive, yet he loves to immerse himself in the 'business' of the group. Coming as he does from the world of pop, he knows all about bad deals and broken dreams. So, quite naturally, he is more wary, and always has questions, whilst being respectful and appreciative of everyone's role in the business. The most fragile and vulnerable of the four, Sébastien can be easily hurt and is very protective of his own and Il Divo's interests. Having had a very rough time in the past, he is extremely kind and considerate and ensures that other people are thanked and remembered.

Urs, for me, is the most trusting. He has never questioned anything I have done, nor brought me to task for anything I have suggested. In fact, I have never had a single argument or awkward moment with him. He is charming, supportive and loyal. A very focused person, Urs keeps his own counsel and speaks only after much deliberation when he has something really important to say. People could – and probably do – label him as aloof or a loner, but that is a total misinterpretation of his character. He is very appreciative of what Il Divo's success has achieved for them all.

The rise of Il Divo has been unprecedented. After their initial appearance on UK television's *Parkinson* on 18 September 2004, their album *Il Divo* went straight to number one in the UK charts, making it the first debut album to reach that spot without a hit single since *Led Zeppelin* in 1969, nearly forty years before. This success was emulated around the world with a further thirteen number ones. *Il Divo* went into the top five in twenty-six countries, and sold five million copies within its first six months of release.

Traditionally, the American market has been notoriously difficult for international artists to break, but Il Divo set out to achieve the impossible from the beginning. On 5 January 2005, *Il Divo* debuted at number four on the main Billboard Album Charts and number one on the Billboard Classical

Chart. This success was accompanied by an appearance on *The Oprah Winfrey Show* and guest spots followed on every influential show in the US – from *The Tonight Show with Jay Leno*, to *Live with Regis and Kelly* and *The Today Show*. Oprah was moved to comment on air: 'I don't know what song those guys were singing, but whatever it was it gave me goose bumps all over.'

In the first half of 2005, they circled the globe promoting their album and introducing themselves to the world through a series of high-profile TV appearances, such as the *Idrettsgalla* award show in Norway, *Wetten Dass* in Germany, *The Logie Awards* in Australia, *Bennissimo* in Switzerland, *Muziekfest* in Holland, *Mezamashi* in Japan and *Miss World* in China.

In the summer of 2005, they recorded their second album, *Ancora*, and this time the release of the album in November of that year was virtually simultaneous around the world. *Ancora* debuted at number one yet again in the UK and led to a performance on *The Royal Variety Show* in front of the Queen. Further prestigious performances such as the *Ondas Awards* in Spain and *Night of the Proms* in France fuelled *Ancora*'s similar success around the globe, with a top five in twenty-one countries, and twelve number ones.

Meanwhile, the release of *Ancora* in the USA was preceded by an album of Christmas songs entitled *The Christmas Collection*, which was America's highest-selling Christmas album that year. *Ancora* followed in January 2006. To coincide with the release of the album, Il Divo

launched their world tour in Wallingford, Connecticut on 31 January, the day the Billboard Album Charts were to be published. As the band was about to walk on stage for their first ever concert, it was my privilege to tell them that *Ancora* had debuted at number one. Il Divo joined Coldplay, the Beatles and Led Zeppelin as one of an elite few British-signed bands to have an album debut at number one on the Billboard Album Charts. Il Divo were breaking new boundaries, exceeding all expectations and making everyone take notice around the world.

Il Divo's tour continued around the USA in early 2006 and then moved on to Australia, the UK and Europe – eighteen countries in all. It was a sell-out, with 500,000 Il Divo fans turning out to the eighty-six dates. A monumental achievement for a band on their first ever tour.

Other highlights of 2006 were Il Divo's recording and performance of the official song of the FIFA 2006 World Cup in Germany and a six-week US tour with Barbra Streisand, who invited them to be her special guests, singing their own songs on stage as well as joining her for three duets. The end of 2006 saw the release of their third album, *Siempre*, and the release of *The Christmas Collection* in many countries around the world, which led to further global chart success, particularly in Canada, where *Siempre* and *The Christmas Collection* occupied the number one and two spots in the weeks leading up to Christmas. Similarly in Spain, *Siempre* held the number-one spot for eight weeks, achieving quadruple-platinum sales and taking the chart tally for the album to a top-three place in nineteen countries.

This success story is obviously, in part, a tribute to the talent and work ethic of the four boys who have adhered to an incredibly gruelling schedule over the past three years, especially the numerous 4.00 a.m. calls in TV studios around the world. However, it would be remiss of me not to acknowledge some key people behind the scenes who have helped and supported Il Divo on this amazing journey. Firstly of course, without Simon Cowell's vision and belief, Il Divo would not exist. I would also like to salute the support and commitment demonstrated by everyone at SYCO Music and Sony BMG, as well as Meredith Plant and Gary Casson, my associates at Octagon. Also, Il Divo's agents: John Giddings (Solo) in the UK and Europe and David Zedeck (CAA) in the Americas, Southeast Asia and Australasia; and the group's concert promoters, including Simon Moran in the UK, Larry Magid and Live Nation in North America, Seirjo Udo in Japan, Paul Dainty in Australasia and numerous others around the world.

In particular, I feel compelled to highlight the role of Sonny Takhar, Managing Director of SYCO Music/TV, whose belief in Il Divo together with his strategic and creative thinking and understanding of what is needed to support and develop Il Divo has been such an important part of this success story.

As I write this foreword, Il Divo are in the middle of their second tour, this time taking in seventy-six dates in thirty countries around the world. The tour, which launched in Kuala Lumpur in January 2007, will conclude in Holland in July. This tour has taken them to many new territories, including Southeast Asia, Japan, South Africa, South America and Canada. Yet in spite of all their tour accomplishments, the journey has only just begun...

I have been fortunate to work with many great artists in my forty years in the music business, including The Rolling Stones, The Who, Duran Duran, Lynyrd Skynyrd and Madness, but I have never been part of anything like this. In three short years, under intense scrutiny, the four members of Il Divo have risen to every challenge, responded to the demands of an incredibly unforgiving industry and fulfilled the dreams of millions of fans around the world. Selling 19 million albums and over 1.5 million concert tickets on six continents is not simply the result of good luck but is testament to a unique talent. The achievement of Il Divo is all the greater when one considers this has all been achieved without radio play, traditionally the most important support platform of our industry.

Il Divo have brought the sound of opera to the masses and spearheaded a whole new musical genre known as 'classical crossover'. Their success has spawned many similar performers and groups – a great compliment – but they have only been imitated, never surpassed. I have no doubt that their achievements will stand the test of time.

IL DIVO
WORLD TOUR 2006
AAA

Carlos

I Do It My Way

For a hot-blooded guy like me, who spends so much of his life on the road, playing the Latin lover, singing romantic songs that arouse passion in others, it was essential that my wedding day should be a day that neither Geraldine nor I would ever forget, and I am glad to say that I achieved that dream. The toughest part was keeping my plans secret from my bride-to-be and coming up with a story that would get her to Disneyland in California, armed with a wedding dress.

'It's a photoshoot for *Hello!* magazine,' I told her over the phone. 'They're doing a feature of all Il Divo's girlfriends dressed up for the biggest day of their lives. So please go out and buy a gown. Dress up like a princess.'

Geraldine, who by then was used to the crazy world that Il Divo live in, didn't suspect anything. She took it in her stride and went out and bought a wedding dress for the photoshoot. And I must say her choice – a lovely ivory satin gown decorated with pearls and embroidery – could not have been more perfect.

Then, on the night before the wedding, my lovely, unsuspecting bride-to-be checked into the presidential suite I had booked at a swanky hotel and waited for me to come back from a concert Il Divo was giving in San Diego.

Around half past one in the morning, feeling incredibly excited about what I was about to do, I stepped through the door, ready to propose. I sat down on the sofa and asked Geraldine to come and sit beside me.

'Geraldine,' I said, 'we've been together such a long time and I love being with you. Would you like to marry me?'

'Oh, *yes*,' she said.

'Okay then,' I said. 'Now I can let you in on my secret. We're getting married tomorrow.'

'Okay then,' I said. 'Now I can let you in on my secret. We're getting married tomorrow.'

'For *real?*' she gasped, truly shocked. Then the floodgates opened and we both cried.

I first met Geraldine, who is half French, half Spanish and a professional singer, when I was playing Marius in *Les Misérables*. We met towards the end of my second year in the show, when Geraldine was in the theatre rehearsing the roles of Eponine and Cosette. After *Les Mis* we appeared in a lot of musicals together. For example, I played Vince and Geraldine played Sandy in *Grease*, in *Peter Pan* I played Captain Hook and she played Peter and in *Beauty and the Beast* she played the Beast and I played Beauty. I jest! It was, of course, the other way around.

I was twenty-three when I got the part of Marius in *Les Misérables* in 1992. It was my first musical and it took about three years of auditioning for me to get the part. I went up for the job so many times. In the beginning I auditioned for Cameron Macintosh and the American team, then later for the English team. By the time I was told I'd got the part of Marius, I'd cooled a bit. My opera career had started to take off and by then I was beginning to think, 'Is this right for me? Should I do it?' But I had fallen in love with the music of *Les Misérables* and so I accepted the offer. I did 685 performances between 1992 and 1994.

I knew from the moment I first set eyes on Geraldine that she was the girl I wanted to spend the rest of my life with. As we continued to work together in various productions and fell more and more in love, I grew ever more certain that she was *the* one for me, and we've been together ever since. She is beautiful – in body, mind and spirit. She has a very gentle, sweet, open personality and great strength of character. I admire her strength and how hard she works. She's not only my lover, she's my twin – truly my other half. It is just unbelievable how in tune we are, how well we know each other. When we are apart I speak to her at least six times a day, which is never enough.

I knew from the moment I first set eyes on Geraldine that she was the girl I wanted to spend the rest of my life with.

Our wedding in Disneyland on 26 June 2006, which I had so lovingly planned, was the best day of our lives, a fairytale come true. I had, of course, flown in my parents, Magdalena and Carlos Snr, along with Geraldine's mother, who is called France. Everyone was in on the secret except the bride.

As I stood waiting under a candlelit gazebo beside Disney's Grand California Hotel for Geraldine to arrive, I was so happy I couldn't stop smiling. The gazebo had been filled with roses and the air was full of their fragrance. Then, as I watched my bride-to-be step down from Cinderella's crystal coach, which had been strewn with flowers and was drawn by horses, my heart just soared. I was so thrilled to have pulled off such an elaborate trick.

The actual service, which was also attended by my fellow Il Divos, David, Sébastien and Urs, along with Mickey and Minnie Mouse, then continued in fairytale style. A footman, dressed in royal blue and white, carried a purple cushion up the aisle bearing our wedding rings, which had been placed in a Cinderella-style slipper. Then my sister, Rosemary, who was Geraldine's matron of honour, walked forward with my nieces, seventeen-year-old Noemi and eleven-year-old Myreya, who were her bridesmaids.

'Hear ye, hear ye,' the cry rang out, as trumpeters heralded Geraldine's arrival. 'Please rise and welcome the love of Carlos's life, the beautiful bride-to-be Geraldine Larrosa.' Then, as the strains of Mendelssohn's 'Wedding March' filled the air, Geraldine, looking incredibly calm for a bride who'd had less than twenty-four hours' notice of her marriage, walked up the aisle escorted by France.

In the middle of the wedding, a barber shop quartet sang for us, which was just great, and at the reception afterwards the white chocolate wedding cake had the words 'And they lived happily ever after' written in gold on it.

I knew Geraldine would appreciate all those touches. Her favourite films when she was a little girl were *Bambi, Dumbo* and *Cinderella* and, like me, she has remained young at heart. I knew just how much the magic of Disneyland meant to her. Soon after we first met in Madrid, we went on a trip to Disneyland Paris and Geraldine had been utterly entranced by a video of Disneyland weddings. 'Oh, how amazing,' she said, 'to have a crystal carriage and everything on your wedding day.' At that moment I thought, 'Carlos, remember that,' and I never forgot it. Some time later, I purchased the Madrid apartment we had rented and shared for seven years. I woke up one morning and said to myself, 'Okay, I have my home now. All I need is my bride. I'm going to ask Geraldine to marry me.'

By then we had been in love and together for fourteen years, but had never found the time to get married. Geraldine was always busy with musical theatre and I was forever flying around fulfilling my operatic commitments. Having made the decision, though, I was determined to see it through. At first I thought we would get married in Las Vegas, when Il Divo had a day off, but then David said, 'Why don't you get married in Disneyland? Geraldine would love that.' 'He's right,' I thought, 'she would. We'll do it there.'

It is lucky that neither Geraldine nor I are jealous by nature, because we spend a lot of time apart. For example, between 26 June 2006, when we got married, and December that year, we only managed to spend twenty-eight days together, and only a few of those were consecutive. The good thing about being in the same business, though, is that we both know what's what and how it works. As a performer in a group like Il Divo, it is essential to feel free to charm people and be kind and generous to those we meet, and Geraldine accepts that. She isn't jealous. She knows that being flirtatious is part of my Latin personality and that I've been like that since I was a child. I *love* flirting. It is part of my performances, both on and off the stage, and she trusts me and accepts that, given my nature, I will, like the song says, 'do it my way'.

Being flirtatious is part of my Latin personality and I've been like that since I was a child. I *love* flirting. It is part of my performances, both on and off the stage

Some interviewers, though, take my larger-than-life flirtatious behaviour on stage seriously and often ask me, directly or indirectly, if I am faithful. 'Oh, yes,' I say. 'I enjoy playing the smouldering, flirtatious Latin lover, but the truth is that I take marriage seriously.'

That really is the truth. I am a very happily married man. I enjoy going out to parties and nightclubs and I love looking at and flirting with beautiful women, but I just look – never touch. And, much to the surprise of the other guys in Il Divo, I will often call Geraldine at four o'clock in the morning, when I get back to the hotel. I can honestly say we are looking forward to a lifetime together – and to starting a family. I love children and want to have some of my own. As I still enjoy childish things myself, I am sure I will be a good father and have a lot of fun with my kids.

These days, Geraldine and I try to see each other at least five days a month, but that is particularly difficult at the moment. She is busy releasing an album in Spain and South America and, if all goes well, it will then be released throughout the world. However often we manage to see each other, it is never enough, and it is an awful wrench when we have to part again. We were young when we met – I was twenty-two, she was seventeen – so have spent the past few years growing up together and have a very special understanding of how each of us feels in any given situation.

But let me backtrack. Although both my parents are Spanish, I was born in Germany, where I continued to live until we moved to Holland and then to Spain. My mother-tongue is Spanish, but I also speak English, German and a little Italian.

The very first time I stepped out on to a stage was in Germany, when I was five and a half years old. There were at least 700 people in the audience and I sang that very famous song 'Granada' in what people said was an amazingly 'mature voice'. I knew then that I would never want to be anything other than a singer.

Despite appearing on stage at such a young age and being so determined to be a singer, I was actually quite introverted as a child. I must have been quite mature for my age, though, because I remember thinking while I was still very young that being withdrawn and distancing myself from people and life wouldn't get me anywhere. Somehow I sensed that if I was to fulfil my dreams, I had to be strong and willing to get out there. Then when I first saw the classic 1951 film *The Great Caruso* about the Neapolitan opera singer Enrico Caruso, whose extraordinarily powerful baritone and later tenor voice made him one of the best-known stars of his time, I knew exactly what kind of singer I wanted to be. In the film the part of Caruso was played by Mario Lanza, another Italian singer who also had a superb voice and became a legend in his lifetime.

Looking back, I can see that my whole life revolved around music – in addition to singing, I also played the piano and guitar – and my family shared my enthusiasm. We only moved to Holland in 1977, when I was eight years old, because a Dutch friend of my parents said, 'I think Carlos has an exceptional voice. Let me take him to Holland and make a recording of him.' Although my dad had a casino business in Germany, he didn't hesitate. He decided to leave the casino in the care of his business partner and moved himself, my mum and my sister to live with me there. So, thanks to the family friend, by the time I was ten years old, I had recorded two singles and an LP, which I still have in my collection at home. The producer at the recording studio was Pierre Kartner, who was very well known in Holland. We continued to live there until my voice broke when I was about thirteen years old. Then we moved to Spain and I went to the Madrid Conservatory to study singing and take piano lessons. While I was at the Conservatory, I took part in several pop competitions and, although I was up against people who were thirty years old, I won my first when I was just fifteen. I never expected to win and I was absolutely amazed when I did.

By the time I was sixteen, I had the kind of voice I have now. People were always saying, 'You could be a Tom Jones if you wanted and sing in a style that would be much more appropriate to your age.' But I didn't falter. I continued going to the Conservatory and spent those years perfecting my singing technique.

When I was still a young man, I remember a medium – a friend of the family – telling me that my maternal grandmother was my guardian angel and that she would always look after me. It was a strange thing to be told, but I have always felt that there is a benign spirit, a loving hand, guiding me through life. I also remember that when I was about twenty-five, a friend showed me an astrological chart. 'It's clear from this,' he informed me, 'that you will not start to become really famous until you are approaching forty.' And he was right.

I recall my grandmother once saying to me, 'If you really want something, Carlos, you *will* get it. You just need to be prepared to work hard.'

I recall my grandmother once saying to me, 'If you *really* want something, Carlos, you *will* get it. You just need to be prepared to work hard.' Whenever I have a really big decision to make, I make a point of remembering her words. I sit alone for a few minutes, close my eyes and consider very carefully what it is I want, what I should do and what will best allow me to live life my way. It works for me. Most of the time I do the right thing. It was like that with Il Divo. When that opportunity knocked at my door, just as I was succeeding in getting good reviews and a reputation in operatic circles, I took myself off for a few quiet moments before making my decision.

My parents have always been very supportive and I've always been very close to them. I've never been ashamed to admit that I was – and am – a mummy's boy. Perhaps that's why Il Divo CDs always sell out around Mother's Day! When I'm away, I ring my mum Magdalena and my dad Carlos at least three times a day. They are so proud of what I have achieved and say things like, 'You're still number one in Spain' or 'Guess what I've been reading about you in the newspaper?'

All in all, I had a fantastic childhood and youth, but I wasn't spoiled. My parents taught me that if I wanted something, I had to work for it. On one occasion, I remember my father saying I could either get a job in a bar, playing the piano and singing in a place where everybody would be smoking (which would have been very bad for my voice), or, if I had the balls, I could work in his casino, giving out change to punters who included among their number some very tough guys – and that was what I chose to do.

My father was pleased about that, thought it was a good opportunity for me to gain experience of people from different walks of life. He also made it very clear that he respected me for not being the sort of guy who was always asking his parents for money. In truth, I always preferred to work for what I wanted, from the age of seven onwards. Whatever jobs I took on, though, I was never tempted to change my long-term plans. I always knew that I would be a singer and couldn't imagine a life without that. It was a burning passion, something I just had to do.

I was never tempted to change my long-term plans. I always knew that I would be a singer and couldn't imagine a life without that. It was a burning passion, something I just had to do.

During my days at the Conservatory, where I attended vocal master classes with the legendary Alfredo Kraus and Montserrat Caballé, I often appeared on TV shows. Between 1989 and 1991 I worked as a singer-cum-presenter on a TV programme before getting the part in *Les Misérables*, which was followed by a lead part in *Man of La Mancha*, where the song 'The Impossible Dream' comes from, followed by *Beauty and the Beast*, which proved to be incredibly hard work.

It was while I was in *Beauty and the Beast*, playing the Beast to Geraldine's Beauty, that I overreached myself and had a really bad accident which took a serious toll on my mental as well as physical health. By that time I was a very confident performer – overconfident, perhaps. I thought I knew myself, knew what I could and couldn't do, both from a singing and acting point of view. But then came the Saturday night performance when I got carried away. The make-up for that show was bad enough – I had so much latex and make-up on my face that I had to spend two and a half hours in the make-up department every single day – but the costume gave me even worse problems. It weighed thirty-five kilos (seventy pounds), which is quite a weight to bear, and during the first act I jumped too high, was borne down by the weight and crashed to the boards. I didn't feel the pain immediately, but I knew that something was broken.

However, as it was a Saturday night and we had a full house, I managed to get to a chair, hauled myself on to it and continued singing. When I reached the point when I was supposed to stand up again, though, I discovered that my ankle was shattered and could no longer bear my weight. I couldn't move. The pain was awful by then, but as I am not the sort of person who could ever bring a curtain down on a performance, and as my next song was the climax of the first act, I struggled on, managed somehow to get through it, then collapsed and was rushed off to hospital.

It was six months – the longest six months of my life – before I was able to return to the theatre. During that time I couldn't walk and the break refused to heal properly. That accident has left me with a lasting legacy. I used to be a good skier, but I can't ski – or run – now. There was worse to come.

When I returned to *Beauty and the Beast,* I was faced with a new dilemma – a dreadful kind of paralysis known as stage-fright. I had never experienced anything so terrifying, and it was so serious that I had to tell the management I was not well, had come back too soon and had to have more time off to recover.

I knew I had to get back on that stage as soon as possible, though. If I didn't, the stage-fright would totally overwhelm and defeat me, and I would have to give up my singing career. When I returned once more there were still some terrible moments to be endured. There were times just before the curtain went up when I just stood frozen-limbed on stage, not able to move a muscle. It was as if I was paralysed. Then, mysteriously, after six weeks of this hell, the stage-fright disappeared as suddenly as it had come, never to return. To this day I don't know what caused it and I don't like thinking or talking about it in case it returns.

Up until that production I had thoroughly enjoyed mixing different musical styles, but after appearing in *Beauty and the Beast* I returned to my first love – opera – and was fortunate

enough to get the part of Marcello in *La Bohème*, which was followed by worldwide acclaim as *primo baritono* in opera roles that included Enrico in *Lucia di Lammermoor*, Sharpless in *Madame Butterfly*, Rodrigo in *Don Carlo*, Figaro in *Il Barbiere di Siviglia*, Germont in *La Traviata* and King Alfonso in *La Favorita*.

I knew I had to get back on that stage as soon as possible, though. If I didn't, the stage-fright would totally overwhelm and defeat me, and I would have to give up my singing career.

The good thing about being in musicals during my early career was that, in many respects, it was like a continuation of my schooldays, a time when I continued to learn lots of things. I still think musical theatre is the most complete form of theatre because you need to be able to act as well as sing in order to hold an audience's attention, and sometimes you are given quite large speaking parts. That training stood me in very good stead when I joined Il Divo because so many of the songs we sing tell a love story and you need some acting skill to be able to do that well. I am very proud of those moments when I succeed in getting across the passion of certain lyrics. For me, it is always more important to be told that I have moved somebody to tears, touched their heart, than to be told that I sang a song really well.

I guess I could say I have lived a charmed life. From childhood onwards, one success has followed another. But that doesn't mean that I have never experienced unhappiness, grief or heartbreak. I first fell passionately in love when I was twelve years old and, just as my feelings for her were at their most intense, she broke my heart and went off with another boy. Since then I have had my heart broken on several occasions and have learned the hard way what it feels like to experience pain, loss and suffering. Those heartbreaks, though, have a plus side. Many arias and songs are about unrequited love, yearning and loss, and my personal heartbreaks have certainly affected how I sing them.

I was singing in Dublin when my manager telephoned to say that a record company wanted me to do an audition, but he had no idea what the audition was for.

I was in for a surprise, followed by a shock. For a start, the audition was being held at the National Concert Hall in Dublin, the same place that I had sung the night before, when my name had been on the hoarding. Then, while I was recovering from this, I saw a very long queue of people, waiting in what I now know to be *X Factor* style, each clutching a number. I had thought I was going for the usual one-to-one audition and my ego was immediately deeply offended. Convinced there must be a mistake, I ignored the queue and went up to the front desk. I gave the receptionist my name, but she just responded by handing me a number and telling me to join the queue.

'You must be joking,' I said, flustered, and went outside to call my manager.

I guess I could say I have lived a charmed life. From childhood onwards, one success has followed another. But that doesn't mean that I have never experienced unhappiness, grief or heartbreak.

'What's going on?' I asked. 'I sang at this theatre yesterday. I'm not going to wait in a queue with hundreds of other hopefuls today.'

Then, still in a huff, I rang Geraldine.

'Calm down, Carlos,' she said. 'Just do it. You never know what might come of it.'

So in the end I swallowed my pride, joined the queue and, when my turn came, sang one aria from the opera *La Favorita*, then the song 'Impossible Dream' from *Man of La Mancha*.

Later that day, after I'd returned to Madrid, my manager called again. 'Simon Cowell would like to have a meeting with you in London,' he said. 'Who's Simon Cowell?' I asked.

When I finished singing, a guy from the record company came over to me and said, 'Are you busy next year?'

'Yes, *very*,' I replied.

'Could you stay another three days?'

'No,' I replied.

'Don't you want to do this?' he asked, surprised.

'Not particularly,' I replied, and, as my feathers were still somewhat ruffled, I left.

Later that day, after I'd returned to Madrid, my manager called again. 'Simon Cowell would like to have a meeting with you in London,' he said.

'Who's Simon Cowell?' I asked. Simon might have been well known in the UK and US, but he was unknown in Spain and I, for one, had never heard of him.

When I went to see him he was very charming and extraordinarily patient. He spent three days trying to convince me that Il Divo was a really good idea. I certainly took some convincing, though. I was not a star-struck hopeful – I was an experienced professional singer who already had an established career. Having met Simon, I went back to Spain to discuss what was on offer with Geraldine and my parents.

'I don't think you should do it,' my dad said. 'It was *really* hard for you to make the change from musical theatre to opera, and I don't think you should risk what you've achieved.'

What my dad meant was that in musical theatre you use a microphone to amplify your voice, but in opera your voice has to be much more powerful and able to reach the back of the stalls and balcony. When you make the transition, it can take a while before you can sing opera without a mike.

IL DIVO
IL DIVO
IL DIVO
SYCOmusic

At that stage, my dad was not alone in advising me to turn down Simon's offer. Lots of my professional contacts said, 'Carlos, you'd be crazy to join a singing group. You'll ruin your opera career.' My mum and Geraldine, however, both said, 'Do it, Carlos. *Do it*.'

In the end, as I was rather bored with the small-mindedness that can be found in the close circle of the opera world, I decided to grab at the chance to do something different. I loved singing opera, but I didn't like all the nonsense that surrounded it. It's a very competitive, incestuous world, full of self-opinionated people and performers who are obsessed with who can sing the loudest, who has the best voice. Throughout my early career, I had too many people around me who I thought were my friends, but who stabbed me in the back. When this happened, I learned to stand on my own two feet and be strong. By nature, I'm a very open person and I'm prepared to give a lot of myself to people, but there were many occasions when I was disappointed and bewildered by other people's reactions.

So, having decided to say yes to Il Divo, I signed the contract and cancelled my future engagements, which included a very prestigious booking to sing at Covent Garden. I really did take a huge risk, and my dad remained very anxious during this time. I was the first person to be chosen for the group, and I'm very glad I made the decision to join up.

When Urs, David, Sébastien and I first met up at the studio our attitude was very much, 'Okay, let's get started and see what happens.' That doesn't mean, however, that it was not very tough in the beginning. I was then – and am now – a perfectionist who will only do something if I can do it to the highest possible standard, and that insistence on doing things my way doesn't make me an easy guy to be around. Also, as we all came from different countries, our early conversations were littered with misunderstandings, which kept sending the tension sky-high.

I am the first to admit that I am typically Latin, a very temperamental guy who can go from 0 to 60 in as many seconds, and I am given to exploding when I see that something is wrong. Once I've exploded and got things off my chest, however, that's that. It might take a few hours to clear the air, but then it's all over. I do not brood or hold grudges. In fact, the good thing about me is that although I go off like a firework, I am very straight and always tell people, however important or famous they are, exactly what I think. So there is no subterfuge, no nasty undercurrents and at least everybody knows where they stand. One problem is that I'm given to swearing all the time in Spanish, but when I curse in English, the same words sound much more offensive. That is not good news. A quartet needs to get on to sing well together.

I found being part of a group very difficult at first. I'd been singing as a soloist for many years and suddenly there I was sharing the stage – and the limelight – with three other voices. Slowly but surely, however, we all learned how to behave like brothers during a performance. I'm sure that growing up with an older sister helped me in this. Like most siblings, she and I used to fight like cat and dog and we would really wrestle with each other, which was bad luck for me as she was into judo, but despite this we learned to accommodate and love each other. I have great respect for other people's talent, and I always knew that once the other guys and I had spent sufficient time together we would get to know what makes each of us tick and what gets under our skins.

> I decided to grab at the chance to do something different. I loved singing opera, but I didn't like all the nonsense that surrounded it.

These days, despite the language problems, I really appreciate the fact that we come from different countries and cultures, and I now believe that if we had all been Spanish the group would not have worked so well. I am a strong believer in destiny and I think it was Il Divo's destiny to be exactly what it is: a mini United Nations of different nationalities. Urs is totally Swiss: everything has to be precise and run on time, just like a good watch, and a note has to be held so long and no longer. David is all American: he's like a big kid, always joking and larking around. He can't keep still, and now that he is learning to play the drums, he is driving us all mad with his twitching. He even jiggles his hands around when he is asleep. Séb's the one I enjoy going out to nightclubs with; we've had some great nights out together. He's a very sensitive guy, and when you misinterpret something he says, you can be sure he will take it personally. He wouldn't hurt a fly, and is very easily hurt himself. Sébastien is *very* French – a bit of a dreamer. He wears his heart on his sleeve and knows how to charm and touch others and dramatize events.

We are all natural-born entertainers who love what we do, and that is why we appreciate the importance of our relationship with each other and why we always rally like brothers after differences of opinion. At the end of the day, although each of us retains our individuality, we work together as a team that has the same aspirations and goals. We are only too aware that people have invested a lot of time and effort in us, and we are only too happy to give back 110 per cent.

EXIT

When we first got off the ground, some people kept saying that we were a 'manufactured group', meaning, I suppose, that our existence was contrived because we were brought into being by Simon. But every group has to have a beginning, and there is nothing fake or manufactured about us. From the moment we came together, we brought the best of all our previous experiences and hard work to what we do. But whatever we did – or said – in those days, the critics still treated us as if were just another boy-band, and interviewers, who knew nothing about our classical training and operatic backgrounds, often said, 'Are you sure you can sing?' Such questions just acted as a spur, though, and made us even more determined to prove we were not just another manufactured group clad in designer shirts and suits. We were for real – serious singers and performers.

Yes, our music is a kind of crossover – and 'popera' is as good a word as any to describe the fact that we treat our songs in a very popular way and finish them in an operatic style – but there's nothing wrong with that. We must be doing something right. Since we came on to the scene, the attention we've received has been quite extraordinary. It's like living in a dream. That moment at the end of a concert when the audience stands up and claps and cheers and whistles is just unbelievable, and one of the highlights for me remains the first time that Il Divo performed live. This was in London, at a place called The Grove. It was a showcase, and all the people from our record company were present. We were all *so* nervous we were shaking.

I have often reminded myself that in the past opera was the pop music of its day, and I see absolutely no reason why romantic songs sung in an operatic style shouldn't rise to the top of the popularity charts again. My reaction to being surrounded by a huge orchestra in front of a vast audience in a packed venue is something that is almost impossible to put into words. I just adore being on stage and using my voice in the best way I know how. No adjective could do justice to the feeling I get when I'm delivering the climax of one of our songs.

We are all agreed that when we started to sing together, we were not at all sure what the end result would be. I'm the baritone of the band, so my voice is a little darker and deeper. David brings in the typical tenor voice, while Sébastien delivers the pop style. Urs contributes a really lovely, mellow middle voice. So that's where we began. We just mixed all our voices together like a cocktail, and – eureka! – this marriage of opera and pop music worked, 'created magic', we were told, for listeners. 'Il Divo,' one of our management team was quoted as saying, 'is more than the sum of its parts. It is a well-balanced, well-oiled machine where every voice has its own strengths.' I liked that.

I just adore being on stage and using my voice in the best way I know how. No adjective could do justice to the feeling I get when I'm delivering the climax of one of our songs.

Our first album, *Il Divo*, released in October 2004, ended Led Zeppelin's forty-year record of being the only band to achieve a number-one album without first issuing a commercial single release, and it was the highest-charting debut album ever for a UK-signed act in America. There was no doubt in our minds that it was 'Regresa a Mi', the Spanish version of Toni Braxton's 'Unbreak My Heart', that first secured for us millions of fans.

We certainly never believed that we would be so successful so soon, and it's still hard for us to take in that it has only been three years since our TV debut singing 'Unbreak My Heart' led to a place in the top five in twenty-six countries for our first album. It was an amazing achievement that confirmed that we had obviously succeeded in finding the right sound.

We all held our breath when our second album, *Ancora*, was released in 2005, and we were overjoyed when it went straight in at number one in the USA, sold a phenomenal 150,000 copies there in just one week and confirmed us as one of the biggest acts in the world. Likewise, *Ancora* went straight to number one in the UK.

Deciding what songs to include on our albums has always been a matter of teamwork. People are always asking if we have serious disagreements about the choice of songs, but I prefer to call them heated discussions. We're four professional guys with strong opinions, so we are bound to have differences from time to time. The record company comes up with a list, then it's decision time for us. For *Siempre*, our third album, released in 2006, we decided to sing everything in Spanish or Italian because those languages suit the operatic voice better and both are considered by many to be the language of love.

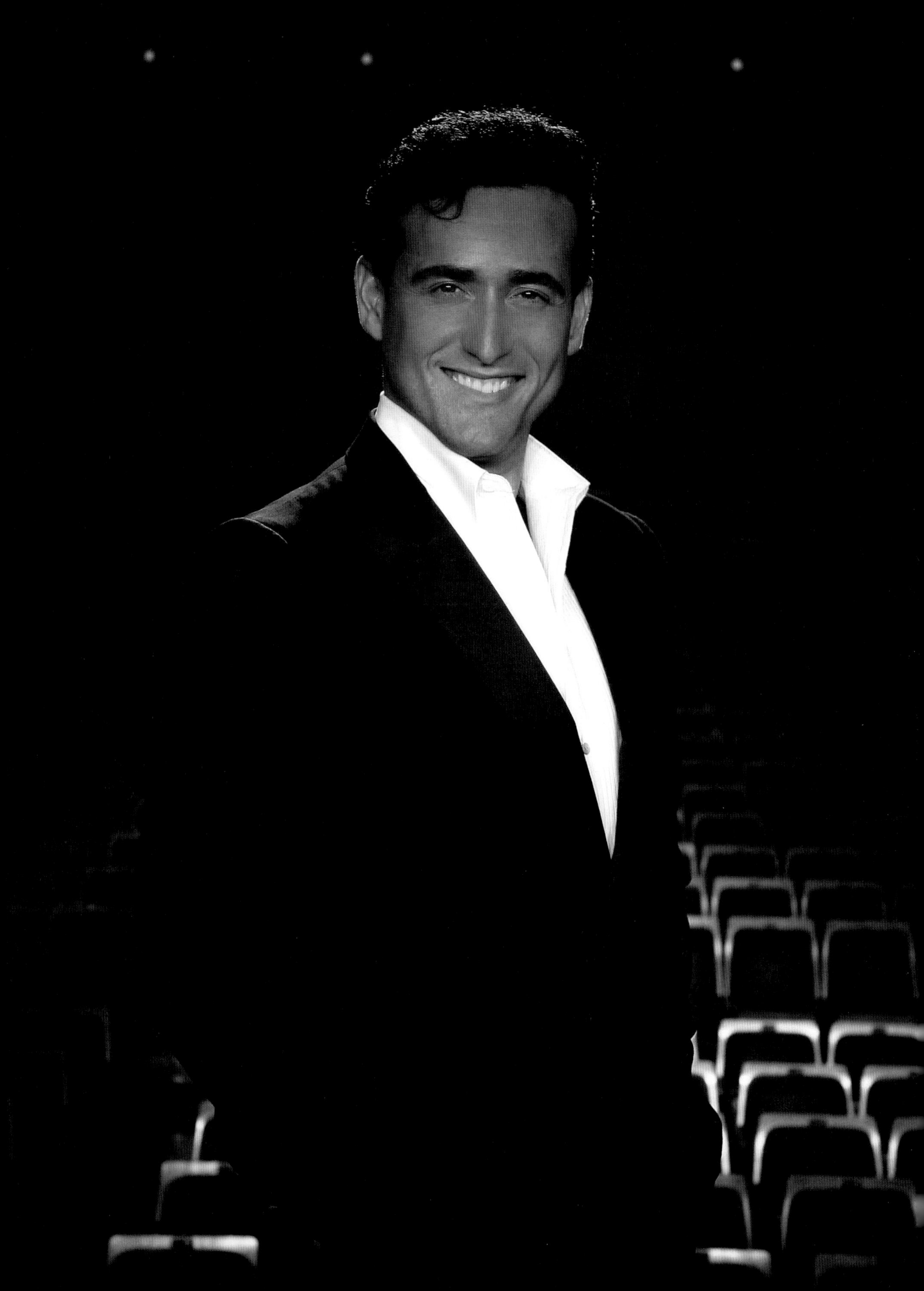

'Siempre' means 'always' in Spanish. I like to sum up our album titles so far in the following way: our first album was entitled *Il Divo*, the second *Ancora*, which means 'again'. So in all we have: Il Divo, again, always – or forever. What we have achieved, therefore, in our titles is a mission statement!

Our first album took three months to record, our second six weeks and our third ten days. Our recordings got easier and easier as we got to know each other's voices better, which part each of us should sing and which language to use for the best effect.

These days, the only time we go into recording studios together is when we are doing harmonies; otherwise, we record separately. After the first album, we realized it would be much less arduous and tiring if we went into the studio one by one, to concentrate on our individual parts. It meant we wouldn't have to keep stopping for someone else to have their turn and it would be easier to get into the swing of things.

Our recordings got easier and easier as we got to know each other's voices better, which part each of us should sing and which language to use for the best effect.

It is still a very exhausting process, however, especially when we wake up in the morning and discover our voices are not in particularly good shape, which can happen from time to time. All in all, we always know we have a really tough time ahead of us when we are recording. We are so lucky, though, to have such fantastic producers. We feel very comfortable when we are recording with Steve Mac, a superb producer who knows our voices better than anybody, supervises everything and is a really great guy to work with. We are also lucky with our Swedish producers, Per Magnusson and David Kreuger. Having such good producers halves the work involved.

In the early days, appearing on television programmes also had its stresses because, although we were often asked to be at the studios incredibly early, we were only ever given one shot at getting our spot right. Nothing much has changed since then, except these days we are invited to the studios so often that some of them have become like second homes, and we are now allowed to arrive much later. The hardest part is not really knowing how the mix of our voices is going to come out, how we are going to sound. Sometimes the studio mikes don't work, sometimes the speakers don't work, sometimes, depending on the studio we are in, the acoustics are not at all good. Sometimes we can't hear each other's voices properly and can end up singing too loudly and drowning out each other. Studio performances are much easier when it's just one guy singing. When there are four, it's a much bigger challenge.

Sébastien and Urs always use ear monitors, but David and I cannot do that because when we go for the high notes they create too much pressure on our ears. We just have to sing in the old-fashioned way, listening to our voices acoustically and hoping for the best.

By far the most satisfying way to perform is live on stage. Nothing beats that. Although we have a management team to guide us, we produce our own shows. We are the ones who put up the money and choose where to do them and what songs to sing. In other words, we are the bosses, which means we can do what we like, what we think is best for our group and our performances. Sometimes we use a stage-set for one venue, then adapt it for another. Likewise, we sometimes change the order of the songs. In fact, we never stop exploring different ways to please our fans.

Interviewers are always asking us how we manage to live a balanced life, especially when we are on tour. All I can say is that it is very difficult. We are often in each other's company for sixteen hours a day while on the road doing promotions, and even though we sometimes travel in the comfort of our own private jet, we still suffer from exhaustion. Being on the road is tough – *really* tough – and doesn't leave much time for anything other than making phone calls home and trying to catch up on sleep. Although I love what I do and would not change it for the world, I really miss Geraldine and my family and friends when we are away. Even this, though, has a plus side. It has taught me how important it is to appreciate whatever precious time we do have together.

If it should ever become too much, though, and my days in Il Divo come to an end, I would like to produce and direct, and take musical theatre to Spain. I know I would enjoy this because earlier in my career I produced a cast recording for the musical *Peter Pan* and loved doing that. I also enjoyed working as a musical director in *Grease*, which involved rehearsing and arranging all the harmonies for the singers. I would also love to give others the benefit of my experience by teaching, especially children and young people. I know from my own experience that there are so many teachers in this world who think they know things when they do not. In all, I had fourteen teachers. Some told me I was a tenor, others that I was a baritone and some said I would never sing opera. What I did in the end was analyse my voice, to try to understand why I could reach some notes and not others, and then I developed my own technique.

Bay Street
304
innovation for results IBM

A very early happy memory is when we appeared at Mall Music at the Warringah Mall in Sydney and sang 'Unbreak My Heart', 'My Way' and 'Mama' before a crowd of over a thousand before signing copies of our album. On that occasion, Philip Spence of Mall's management team was kind enough to say that while we were doing the signing we were 'gracious, approachable and only too happy to chat with the crowd'. We appreciated that compliment because it revealed how we felt about our fans then, and how we feel about them now. We were also told by Philip that an eighty-one-year-old lady, Berta Cunic, had been waiting to see us since nine-thirty in the morning. That really touched our hearts.

Yet another occasion that stands out in my memory was when our first show in Barcelona coincided with Barcelona playing Arsenal. Barcelona supporters are fanatical and when we arrived we heard that one of Spain's most successful singers had cancelled a performance that night out of fear that nobody would turn up. We were not deterred. There were seventeen thousand people in the audience as we opened our show with 'Unbreak My Heart'. People don't usually sing along with us at concerts, but on that occasion we had fourteen- and fifteen-year-old girls doing just that during every song. It was like a pop concert. Before we went on, I asked the promoters to let me know each time Barcelona scored a goal, so that I could announce it to the audience, and at the end of the concert the whole audience sang the Barcelona team's anthem. It was an amazingly moving experience.

> We were so excited about all this, just knew it was an experience we would never forget, one which would give us so many memories to look back on in years to come. It was a time when we were able to show the people out there that we really could sing and perform live.

The year 2006 was another fantastic year for us, even better than our first year, as we spent so much of it performing live on stage throughout a debut world tour which consisted of eighty-six dates in venues in the UK, USA, Europe and Australia. We played to over 500,000 fans; there wasn't an empty seat at any of the venues.

We were so excited about all this, just knew it was an experience we would never forget, one that would give us so many memories to look back on in years to come. It was a time when we were able to show the people out there that we really could sing and perform live. I thrive on the energy a live audience gives me – it is like an electric current passing right through me. That is what life is all about for me, being out there on stage, giving and receiving. It is where I truly come alive, feel at home and am totally happy.

Yet another lovely Il Divo moment took place on 31 January 2006, which happened to be the very first night of our 2006 live tour. Just before the show, as we were getting dressed in our suits, our manager, Peter Rudge, came into the dressing room and said, 'Guys, I have just been informed that you are number one in the Billboard Chart in America.' That was an unbelievable moment for all of us. We felt on top of the world for days.

Another moment I recall during that year was when we were doing an interview for a Glasgow radio station. Dave Marshall, the presenter, introducing us by saying, 'It was only in October 2004 when you four young men came into our radio station with your debut album. Since then you really have conquered the world, not in a volcanic, James Bond sort of way, but by achieving twenty-six number-one chart positions internationally, selling over thirteen million albums and achieving, in America, the highest ever chart debut album for a UK act. Whenever I see press releases about you "conquering the world" it always gives me that image of a man stroking a white cat and saying, "This time next year I will dominate all the world's popular music charts."'

That is what life is all about for me, being out there on stage, giving and receiving. It is where I truly come alive, feel at home and am totally happy.

I enjoyed that moment. It occurred at a time when events were moving so fast that we had had very few moments in which to absorb what was happening, and it was only in that studio, listening to Dave, that I was able to take in what we had achieved – and the James Bond imagery made me laugh.

I was so thrilled when I heard that we were going to record 'The Time of Our Lives' with Toni Braxton, and that the song was to be used as the official 2006 FIFA World Cup anthem and performed at the championship's opening ceremony and the final. Toni, the six-time Grammy Award-winning rhythm and blues singer, has an amazingly husky, sultry voice and was the first singer to release 'Unbreak My Heart' in Spanish and English, a song that was written for her by Diane Warren and which later became so instrumental in our early success. She is just such a sweet, sexy girl, and I can honestly say that we did have the time of our lives performing that song with her. That World Cup, which was won by Italy, was one of the most watched events

in television history. Its viewers apparently numbered almost thirty billion over the course of the tournament, and some sports writers claimed it was the best World Cup ever. We like to think we had a part to play in that!

There was soon to be yet another thrill in store for us.

Soon after I joined Il Divo, Geraldine, who was a huge fan of Barbra Streisand, said to me, 'Wouldn't it be fantastic if you got to sing with Barbra?' and the very thought was enough to send me off in a daydream. Then, one day, when we were at Universal Studios in Los Angeles doing our first show on the live tour, a man introduced himself to us saying, 'Hi guys, I'm Barbra Streisand's manager. She's a huge fan of yours and would love you to come back to the States and share a stage with her.'

That, I can tell you, was one dream I'd never expected to come true. I was not disappointed. Being on tour with Barbra in 2006 was an unbelievable honour that proved to be a fantastic experience for all of us. Of course, we were nervous, but she turned out to be a sweet woman and we couldn't believe she was asking for our opinions. She has a beautiful voice. My only sadness is that we didn't have the chance to spend as much time as I would have liked getting to know her. What with rehearsals and promoting our new album, *Siempre*, we were all just too busy. But it was fantastic being with Barbra on stage. As well as performing our own songs, we also sang three duets with her.

A truly memorable evening was when the Clintons came to one of the concerts. 'Hey guys,' Hillary said, 'you're fantastic. I have all your albums. Bill should play sax with you.'

We also had fleeting glimpses of Lauren Bacall, Sting, Tony Bennett and Robert de Niro during that tour, and although those moments were over in a flash, it was just wonderful to see these world-renowned stars in the flesh.

So many extraordinary things have happened to us that nothing really surprises me any more, but that doesn't mean I've become blasé or take things for granted. I'm still like a child, with eyes as big as saucers, and I don't think anything will ever change that. We do get asked to do some very strange things, though. Often, for example, our fans ask us to autograph their boobs and bums. When one fan got her nipple out, I just thought, 'Oh, okay.'

I suppose it's my fault that we get knickers thrown at us on stage. This doubtless stemmed from an occasion when we were asked during an interview who our favourite singers were. 'Mine is Tom Jones,' I replied. Then, just for fun, I added, 'But I don't know if that is because he has a great voice or because women chuck their knickers at him.' Ever since then, fans have thrown their knickers at us – and, provided they're clean, I love it. One pair from M&S even had the girl's phone number written inside. When it comes to women expressing their appreciation by throwing their underwear, though, no one will ever beat Tom Jones's record.

I've been a fan of Tom Jones since I was a child and have all his albums and recordings at home. And, joy of joys, when we were singing at Radio City in New York, I learned that he was appearing at the Kodak Theatre, and I was lucky enough to get a ticket for the performance.

When I went backstage to meet him, I couldn't wait to tell him I was a huge fan of his, that he was my hero. We spoke for several minutes, but, idiot that I am, I didn't think to get my photograph taken with him or ask him for his autograph. I only thought of that afterwards when it was too late. It really was a dream come true and it was over far too soon. It's only when you meet very famous people, like Tom Jones, that you realize just how normal they are. He really is a very nice guy. He had heard of Il Divo. Gary Wallis, our musical director and drummer, had worked with him several years back and had told Tom all about us and mentioned that I was a great fan of his and was hoping to meet him one day. Now that I have, I can't wait to meet him again.

One of the loveliest things about becoming well known yourself is that you can get permission to go backstage and meet people on occasions like that. It's one of the perks of the job. I've always thought how strange it is, though, that precisely at the moment you become financially secure – and can afford to pay for what you want – you get offered so many things for free. You also soon realize that you no longer need to wait in line for a restaurant table and restaurateurs will even invite you to come and visit. The more you have, it seems, the more you are given. Another strange thing about becoming a success was that I suddenly discovered I had more friends than I'd ever had before – and some were friends I hadn't seen or heard from for twenty-five years! It's sad, isn't it, when people only want to know you because you have become successful?

When we went to Tokyo during our 2007 world tour, the audience was unnervingly well behaved and polite to begin with. Throughout the concert they hardly made a sound and when they did clap it was very quietly and slowly. That, however, was not to last! When we moved forward and sat on the edge of the stage to sing 'Somewhere', the last song of the evening, the audience suddenly erupted and went berserk. Having leaped out of their seats, they rushed towards us, screaming their heads off, and we found ourselves witnessing a potentially dangerous situation. In the crush, one woman became sandwiched between David and myself, and as the mass of people behind her continued to push forward, her head was forced down onto David's knee. Even then, although she could hardly breathe, she still kept gasping, 'I love you. I love you.' We were really worried. We could see she was slowly turning blue and, for a moment or two, until the crowd drew back and the situation sorted itself out, we were afraid she would get seriously hurt.

I've always thought how strange it is, though, that precisely at the moment you become financially secure – and can afford to pay for what you want – you get offered so many things for free.

There were similar overwhelming reactions in Colombia during that tour. All day and even late at night, people waited outside our hotel, hoping to see us leaving or arriving. In the end, we couldn't leave our rooms between shows because we would have been mobbed by the fans waiting outside.

The whole South American tour was an unbelievable experience. We had been to Mexico before, but not to some of the other countries, such as Chile, Colombia and Argentina. In Chile, for example, when we were in the middle of singing 'Without You', a fan suddenly ran down the aisle, climbed on to the stage, threw herself on the floor, wrapped her arms around Sébastien's leg and just wouldn't let go. When the security guy arrived just seconds later, it was almost impossible for him to release her and we just had to go on singing as if none of this was happening. It was such a relief for Séb – and the rest of us – when he eventually prised her off and led her away. In fact, throughout the entire South American tour the audiences were so enthusiastic we couldn't make a move without being mobbed, and the fans continued to wait outside our hotels until the early hours of the morning.

We had been on the road several times before, doing concerts and promoting our albums, but it was only when we got the kind of reception we did in South America and Asia that it began to dawn on us that we had entered a different league, had become stars. The venues for the concerts were getting bigger and bigger all the time and the screams louder and louder. For the first time, it became necessary for us to change our names when checking into hotels. Before we did that, people were finding out where we were staying and were telephoning us from different time zones at five or six o'clock in the morning.

'I am a fan of yours,' they would say, when, still half asleep, I answered the phone. 'Yes, thank you. I love you,' I would reply, yawning, 'but do you know what time it is?'

There is no doubt about it, things changed for us during that tour, and we started to lose what little privacy we had left. Sometimes, during those days, it was almost overwhelming. I used to enjoy going out to nightclubs after our concerts, but I am seldom able to do that anymore. I'm not really complaining, though, because I realize it is all part of being a success in the business we are in, and, in truth, I'm delighted that we are now such big stars.

As for the future, we just want to grow and grow, and we do our best every single day to improve ourselves. Even my English is improving. Now when I go back to Spain, I sometimes find I am thinking in English and English words come out with the Spanish.

But that doesn't mean I don't still trip up during interviews – put my foot in it, as the English are fond of saying. This happened to me in Australia with the word 'successful'. Just at a moment when I was feeling really tired and jet-lagged, the television presenter asked me how I thought my life had changed since becoming part of Il Divo.

'Well, for a start,' I replied, stifling a yawn, 'I never expected to have so much s-s-suck-sex.'

As she gasped, then started to fall about laughing, and the rest of the group joined in, it took me a moment or so to absorb what I had said, then even I had to laugh.

From that day on, that mistake has followed me to every country we've performed in, as a running joke with the guys. In any case, I think we are all overwhelmed by our SUCCESS and look forward, hopefully, to much more!

David

Somewhere a Place For Us

When I was eight years old, my parents packed all our stuff into some removal vans and we headed off in true frontier wagon style to Colorado. As the last van left San Diego, where I was born, they didn't know if they would ever see any of their possessions again. You see, at that time circumstances had become so hard for the family that we actually didn't even know if we would make it to the planned destination. We only had about seventy dollars left to our name. But Lady Luck was on our side. When we stopped off at Las Vegas en route, my dad put a quarter in a slot machine and fifty bucks came tumbling out. If that hadn't happened, we wouldn't have got to Denver, Colorado. We would have had to stay right there in Vegas and my life would have turned out very differently.

My parents were very traditional; we were a *Leave It to Beaver* kind of family. My dad graduated from the Naval Academy as an engineer and had a twenty-year career in the Navy, eventually rising to the rank of Lt. Commander, and my mom chose to stay home and raise me and my sisters. When my dad retired, my parents invested all their time and money into creating a chair designed to help bathe children with disabilities. Due to several unfortunate circumstances, they got into serious financial difficulties, having sunk everything they had into this invention. But they held strong – they would do anything to feed and house the family – and once we got to Colorado, my father marched straight to an engineering company to try to get a job.

After a lengthy interview, the boss said that he was very sorry, but they didn't have a position to offer him that fit his qualifications and my dad's heart sank.

I guess those early years must have been quite traumatic for me, because I don't remember much before the age of eight, when we made that move to Colorado.

'However,' the boss added, emerging from behind the desk so that my father could see he was in a wheelchair, 'because you have taken such an interest in people with disabilities, I'm going to create a position for you. If you are willing to study hard to get up to speed on robotics, I'll take you on.' And that's what my father did. In my eyes, he proved himself a hero by pulling us out of trouble and making sure we never lacked a roof over our heads and food on the table again.

I guess those early years must have been quite traumatic for me, because I don't remember much before the age of eight, when we made that move to Colorado. I just recall bits and pieces, like how we had to move every couple of years because of the Navy, and that by the time my dad returned to civilian life in 1980, times were hard and it was very difficult for him to rejoin the work force in California. My sister was an ice-skater at the time, a good one, with the potential to go pro, so in fact the move to Colorado was not a random choice. My parents picked it not only for the potential job opportunities, but also because the Olympic training centre was only a couple hours away in Colorado Springs.

Even after we began to call Denver home, however, there were still circumstances that forced us to keep moving around the city, roughly every two years, so I never really settled into a core group of friends. Once we stopped moving around, when I was about twelve, I quickly discovered that it's really hard to gain entry into a gang of friends at that age because they are

IL DIVO
Sydney Entertainment Center
Sydney

already so tight-knit and established. And besides, I was a bit of a loner, an independent kid, and was used to living in my own imagination. Throughout my childhood I remember being very quiet, although my sisters – one six years older and one four years younger – might disagree with me on that. In particular, I recall being very restless, very curious and drawn to the obscure. Whatever it was that the other kids were doing, I didn't want to do that. Inevitably, this meant that I always annoyed those very groups of which I wanted to be a part. I was the one they came looking for because they thought I was too big for my britches and wanted to cut me down to size. The bullying was more psychological than physical, though, because I was tall for my age, bigger than most of them, and whenever I felt them on my heels, I just kept moving. By the time I was in high school, I was used to being thought of as an oddball, a geek, a nerd, because I loved singing in the choir, enjoyed drama class and got roped into musicals. Being a geek never did me any harm. If anything it set me up for the rest of my life!

Whatever it was that the other kids were doing, I didn't want to do that. Inevitably, this meant that I always annoyed those very groups of which I wanted to be a part.

I don't look back on those days with any kind of anger or regret. In fact, I try not to look back on anything with regret. It's all a part of what got me to where I am now. Everything that happens to us contributes to who we are, and we can learn a great deal from both positive and negative experiences. My approach is to take what's positive from any experience, so I can keep moving forward.

I've always had a deep emotional bond with my family and, looking back, I am fully aware that my upbringing was definitely a team effort on the part of my parents. I feel very lucky that they were always so supportive of us kids and tried their best to accommodate the things in which we took interest. Whether it was camping with the Cub Scouts, or taking me to band practice on Saturday mornings when I was learning the trombone, or getting up at four in the morning to take me to swim-team practice, whatever it was, they were there for me, and it's because of their encouragement that I developed an inner strength that kept me on my path and kept me moving forward along it.

Singing wasn't my first musical love. I decided to try my hand at the drums when I was about six, but I broke my arm just before the Christmas I was to receive them. In my frustration at only being able to play one-handed, I put a drumstick right through the snare. And though I cried and said that I was sorry, my parents taught me the lesson that some things you just can't take back. I had broken my drums and I had to live with that.

I moved onto piano lessons, but that was just before the move to Colorado, so they were short-lived. Then, once we had settled in Denver, when I was eight, I started playing the trombone. This was the instrument that suited me best, even though the thing was almost bigger than I was. I decided to really go for it and had private lessons. After a few sessions, my teacher recommended that I audition for the first level of a youth orchestra he knew of. Even though I was technically two years too young, they let me try out for it at my teacher's request. I made the audition and my appetite for music started to grow rapidly. Within a year, I was playing first chair in the third level with high school students. At ten years old, I switched from classical trombone to jazz, as I found it more challenging, still maintaining first chair in a college-level group.

Even though I always loved music, my first choice of career in those days was to be an astronaut.

But even though I always loved music, my first choice of career in those days was to be an astronaut. I have always had a fascination with astronomy. I even had a telescope (no, not to spy on the neighbours!). Twenty-five years ago, there were always clear night skies in Colorado during the summer and you could see so many stars. Not so much any more, now that Denver is no longer a one-and-a-half-horse town. I think part of the reason I was so interested in becoming an astronaut is because they do things that only a handful of people have ever done. That has always been my thing: taking, as Robert Frost wrote, 'the road less travelled by'. I also took one of my dad's colourfully inspirational sayings to heart: 'Better to shoot for the stars and miss than shoot for a pile of s*** and be right on target!'

By the time I got to high school, my interest in the trombone had dropped away and I hadn't seriously taken up another instrument. Instead, I joined the choir. As far as I was concerned, it was just an easy A. What I hadn't counted on was the choir teacher. He was a complete tyrant of the first order and commanded his class as such. But oddly enough, I found this inspirational in a way; I found myself trying to live up to his self-professed unrealistic expectations of perfection. In my sophomore year, he asked me to audition for the male chorus, which I did. They gave me the part of Rooster in *Annie*. The following year, I auditioned again and they gave me the lead part of Noah in *Two by Two*. In my senior year, I played Frederic in Gilbert and Sullivan's *The Pirates of Penzance*.

By this time I had spent so much time on music and the theatre that my grades had slipped very far from where they would have needed to be to get into the Air Force Academy, the first step in my plan to become an astronaut. Therefore, I decided that music was to be my new path and sought out a voice teacher. She helped me realize that although I didn't know exactly what kind of music I would eventually gravitate to, whether it would be music theatre or opera or even jazz or pop, I should get a classical training. She prepared me to audition for the Oberlin Conservatory, and fortunately I made the cut. I started there as a freshman in 1991.

It was during my second year at the Conservatory that I found the music that was to alter my life course more than once over the following thirteen years, when my roommate put on a recording of Puccini's *La Bohème*. I had never heard it before, and Pavarotti's rendition of 'Che Gelida Manina' was stunning. I mean, I was literally stunned into silence, which doesn't happen very often with me. It was at that point that I decided that opera was to be my career. Nothing more, nothing less. It was a seminal moment that inspired me to practise the aria until I was good enough to go to my singing teacher and say, 'This is what I want to do. I want be an opera singer, and I want to sing *La Bohème*.'

Pavarotti's rendition of 'Che Gelida Manina' was stunning. I mean, I was literally stunned into silence, which doesn't happen very often with me. It was at that point that I decided that opera was to be my career.

His face screwed up tight and he was trying very hard to point the corners of his mouth downwards in disapproval or maybe annoyance, but his response was really more bemused than annoyed. I don't think he was used to nineteen-year-old sophomores who knew so clearly what they wanted to accomplish.

After a pregnant pause, he began to explain that opera was a possible end result of a classical training, and not a place to start from. My position was unaltered, and I guess I must have shown a level of confidence in myself that made him curious.

'Alright then. Show me.'

I did.

As I remember it, after I'd finished, he took a minute to think. He shook his head from side to side, as if to say 'no'. But then a chuckle escaped him.

'Well,' he said, 'it's clear that this is what you want, and it's clear that you have the capability, but I still want you to focus on your song repertoire for studio class. Maybe once a month we can make time to work on operatic arias.' Only something you *really* want, something you are born to do, can give you the kind of confidence – some would say arrogance – that I displayed that day. And that's how it was.

By my junior year, once a month had turned into once a week and I was playing leads in opera productions and performing in summer opera programmes like the Utah Festival Opera and Wolf Trap. By the end of my senior year, I had learned and/or performed fifteen leading roles. I stayed at Oberlin for a fifth year to really consolidate my training and received a Masters in Opera Theatre.

> Early on in my singing career, I was accused of being an over-thinker . . . There's always been a very serious side to my character; I've always had a huge sense of responsibility towards my music.

For the next ten years, my career spanned forty-five different operatic and musical parts, from Edgardo in *Lucia di Lammermoor* to the title roles of *Werther* and *Mitridate*, in North America, South America, Australia and Europe.

Early on in my singing career, I was accused of being an over-thinker. In Pittsburgh, during my apprenticeship with the Pittsburgh Opera, my Argentinian teacher/mentor used to say, 'It's not your fault, David, you are an Anglo-Saxon. You live here' – pointing to his head – 'but opera is here' – thumping his heart. 'You are what you are. You can't help it.' The criticism was doubtless fair. There's always been a very serious side to my character; I've always had a huge sense of responsibility towards my music.

However, this comment made me determined to engage my heart as well as my head. I've always been very fortunate in that, thanks to my early training, I've never had to worry about technique when I'm singing. For me, the voice is not the mystical thing that some voice teachers dress it up to be. I instinctively know what my voice is doing at every moment, and this leaves me free to take on board other things, such as engaging my feelings.

This is easier said than done, however. I spent the majority of my operatic career trying to find a way to get in touch with my emotions. The first time they really kicked in was when I performed Tony in Leonard Bernstein's *West Side Story* at La Scala in Milan. It was my first music theatre role since high school, and it reminded me why I love musicals so much. There is more of a balance of drama and the voice, as opposed to opera, where generally the voice is given absolute preference. That experience reshaped the way I thought about singing and the different ways that the operatic voice could be used to touch people. For the first time since high school, I felt the music rather than thinking about it.

It was my first music theatre role since high school, and it reminded me why I love musicals so much. There is more of a balance of drama and the voice, as opposed to opera, where generally the voice is given absolute preference.

After that, I began to think that maybe it was possible that opera had been severely limited by hundreds of years of vocal tradition, and that maybe it needed a booster shot in the form of higher levels of acting, drama and emotional engagement. So I began to try to take what I had learned from *West Side Story* and apply it to my other opera roles. (How's that for logicalizing emotions?) Soon after, I had the wonderful opportunity to audition for Baz Luhrmann, and this turned into one of the highest points of my musical career, when at long last I achieved my dream to play Rodolfo in his production of *La Bohème*, which opened on Broadway in December 2003.

From the very first rehearsal, it was clear that everyone was on the same page: opera could be so much more than a standard tearjerker where the music was enough to hopefully move the audience. We wanted to go a huge step further and tear their hearts out, throw them on the floor and stomp on them (metaphorically of course). We practised with no singing at all for almost two weeks. We made it into a straight drama by translating the Italian libretto into our own language – English for most of us and Russian for the soprano in the cast – and then rewriting the archaic phrasing to give it a more modern and natural feel. The result was a deeper connection to the words and a greater understanding of how and why Puccini's music is so intricately connected with those words, and that had a profound effect on the audience. When the day comes that I go back to opera, I will take this approach for every role.

I have much to be thankful for with regard to that production of *La Bohème*. It is thanks to that opera that there is someone very special in my life right now. She was the understudy for the role of Mimi. During a rehearsal of the scene where Mimi and Rodolfo meet, our eyes locked and something magical happened. I can't find the words to explain what actually happened; suffice it to say that I knew my life was forever changed.

After *Bohème* closed, rather unexpectedly, I went back to traditional opera, which led me to be in Paris at exactly the right time for the audition for Il Divo. Fortunately, my 'Mimi' had the time to come to Paris and be with me for a couple of weeks. We visited Montmartre and Notre Dame, the Eiffel Tower and the Louvre, but we spent most of our time in the Latin Quarter, where *La Bohème* actually takes place, pretending to live as Mimi and Rodolfo. Luckily for us, she didn't have TB, so we didn't have to worry about a tragic ending.

It is thanks to that opera that there is someone very special in my life right now. She was the understudy for the role of Mimi. During a rehearsal of the scene where Mimi and Rodolfo meet, our eyes locked and something magical happened.

These days she travels with me whenever possible, which is wonderful because life is so much happier and simpler when we're together.

I was the last one to join Il Divo. As I mentioned, I happened to be in Paris, working at the Opera Bastille, when I got a call from the assistant director of ... wait for it ... yep, you guessed it ... *La Bohème*. She explained to me that a record company was looking for opera singers who were interested in not singing opera. By this time, I was so enmeshed in the idea of using the classical voice to reach people in new and interesting ways that I had to at least try for it.

I went in to the audition prepared to sing an aria from the opera *Werther* and 'Summertime' from *Porgy and Bess*. I figured the latter was unusual and crossover enough, since it was music theatre and a song traditionally sung by a woman. While I was sitting there, another guy showed up and sat down next to me. It was Sébastien. At that point, I was summoned to the audition room. I sang my pieces and they asked me a few questions about what I thought of crossover music and such, and then they said they would be in touch. When I came out, Séb was looking at me with astonishment in his eyes.

'I think I come to the wrong place,' he said, in a much thicker French accent than he has now.

'What do you mean?' I asked.

'I can't sing like you do.'

I told him that he should go in and just be himself because I didn't know any more than he did what it was that they were looking for. He went in and played and sang the song 'Caruso' and I thought at that point that *I* had come to the wrong audition.

After that came the callbacks, which meant a series of trips on the Eurostar to London, to the studio of the producer we were going to work with. That's where I met Urs and Carlos and found Séb waiting there as well. We began work on the tracks 'Feelings' and 'A Moment Like This'. The record company decided that we were the right blend of voices and temperaments for the job and we were put to the task of creating a record we could all be proud of.

It was then that they filled me in on who was really behind the project: a certain Mr Simon Cowell. I discovered I was the only one in the group who had heard of Simon. Apparently, neither 'Pop Idol' nor the American version of it had ever been aired in France, Spain or Switzerland.

It was then that they filled me in on who was really behind the project: a certain Mr Simon Cowell. I discovered I was the only one in the group who had heard of Simon. Apparently, neither *Pop Idol* nor the American version of it had ever been aired in France, Spain or Switzerland. Since it made no difference to them that the man that everyone loved to hate was heading up our project, I decided it shouldn't bother me either. And as it turned out, we were right not to worry.

Simon is no fool. He's aware that people tune in to see him make cutting remarks, so he gives them exactly what they want, and I think he even enjoys making people hate him. In reality, though, he's a good guy, very down-to-earth. He never made us feel like he was the boss; he never had a 'you will do what I say' attitude. He made us feel we were all part of a creative team working towards the same goals. He always speaks his mind clearly and concisely, and for him everything is black and white. He either absolutely loves or absolutely hates something. There's nothing in between. I have nothing but respect for him.

What I quickly realized was that this project was not going to be what I thought it was. You see, in the opera world, when you make a recording of a show or some arias or whatever, you maybe spend a few days rehearsing and then a couple of days recording to get all the right takes, and then you're done and you move on to something else. I was expecting the same kind of thing, but I couldn't have been more mistaken.

I was asked by Simon to cancel all my opera engagements indefinitely . . . about four years' worth of contracts around the world.

In fact, I was asked by Simon to cancel all my opera engagements indefinitely, which at that time meant about four years' worth of contracts around the world, including my Metropolitan Opera debut. It was really a hefty decision to leave my entire career behind. The music Il Divo was to sing had to have just the right balance of pop and opera, we were told, and that was not going to happen overnight. Simon loved the sound of Andrea Bocelli's voice and the combined power of the voices of the Three Tenors, but he made it clear that he hated the music they performed. Therefore, we had to find our way using only pop material.

I remember that there were more than a few times during the 'experiment' when I thought, 'Did I *really* give up my opera career for this?' We attempted songs in English, Spanish and Italian, to see which language would fit best, but with only moderate success. Then we were presented with Toni Braxton's hit 'Unbreak My Heart'. We were very curious to see how a woman's anthem would work when sung by four men. At first, we tried singing it in English, but it sounded way too feminine, then we tried it in Spanish and everything somehow clicked. When we listened to the mix of 'Regresa a Mi', we all felt the hairs on the back of our necks stand on end, and we knew we had found the sound of Il Divo.

We attempted songs in English, Spanish and Italian, to see which language would fit best, but with only moderate success.

We all thought this new approach really worked and we went back to some of the previous songs and redid them in that style. When they played us the finished album, I thought, 'Yes! This could really be something special!'

If I am honest (and hopefully I don't sound arrogant when I say this), I feel that I have always been the optimist of the band, and if I'm *really* honest, then I have to say I'm not really surprised at the success we have enjoyed. That isn't to say it was easy. It has never been easy. Not one single step was ever taken without some kind of setback or drama, especially at the beginning, when we were trying to put our first album together. But after the breakthrough idea to record 'Unbreak My Heart' in Spanish, I knew we had stumbled upon what I can only describe as 'it'. 'It' is that something that cannot really be defined. It's that element of magic that makes something stand out as truly special. I knew at that point that if we kept working as hard as we were to find the 'it' of every song, every performance, every single moment, then we would hit the pop world like a sledgehammer.

Later, when we started to perform 'Regresa' on TV shows, their switchboards lit up every time, and sometimes even jammed. I thought, 'You know, this really could go to number one'. When it actually did, however, it was still a phenomenal shock to all of us because although everyone had high hopes, you can never *really* be sure that it will happen. Despite the shock, however, I was laughing to myself and thinking, 'I knew it, I knew it!'

It's difficult to put Il Divo into a category of music because there is no pre-existing box to stuff us into. We've been described as 'pop opera', but I think 'operatic pop' would be a more correct description of what we do.

If I am honest (and hopefully I don't sound arrogant when I say this), I feel that I have always been the optimist of the band, and if I'm *really* honest, then I have to say I'm not really surprised at the success we have enjoyed.

During our publicity rounds, we never told anyone we were singing opera. We just said we sing in an opera style, but our material is plainly pop. But as opera was my first love in terms of singing, I always hoped there would be people who heard us who would be moved to make the crossover and go to an opera – and that is exactly what has happened.

Predictably, there was some gnashing of the teeth by the critics, but I believe it was less to do with our music and more to do with the fact that no one knew how to perceive us. Our music couldn't be reviewed as pop or opera, so it was just labelled as 'cheesy'. But our repertoire brought together a lot of different styles of music and there were clearly many people out there who were open-minded enough to appreciate that.

I looked at it this way: nobody had ever done the type of singing that we were doing, and the techniques we combined were ones that all four members of the group could use to share lead vocals throughout a song, beginning in a way that was too delicate to be heard in an acoustic operatic setting and culminating in soaring choruses and finales with real operatic flair. In that way, we succeeded in reaching millions of people with music that had elements within it reminiscent of classical music.

We all knew from the start that some in the opera world would not want their art disturbed and that for them it would be like taking Mona Lisa and dressing her up in a miniskirt. Therefore, we never touch the operatic repertoire. Our aim was to create something completely new and exciting, and if we succeeded in moving people, well, we all agreed we would be more than happy about that.

We wanted to make our kind of music popular all over the world, wanted to touch people of every race, creed and colour. We especially wanted to sing our hearts out for people who wanted an extra surge of romance in their lives. As far as we were concerned, that's what music is all about: transcending barriers, touching people's hearts, transporting them to another place, just through the power of the human voice.

We all knew from the start that some in the opera world would not want their art disturbed and that for them it would be like taking Mona Lisa and dressing her up in a miniskirt. Therefore, we never touch the operatic repertoire.

From the start, Il Divo was – and remains – a democracy. There's no lead singer in our group. We all share the leads and work in harmony with each other – and that's cool.

I'd describe myself as a typical middle child, doubtless because I *was* a middle child. I remember always feeling like the go-between in my family when I was growing up, and the same thing is true in Il Divo, especially at the beginning.

I was definitely the go-between when it came to overcoming the language barriers. As we had all decided that English was going to be our main language of communication (luckily for me), it meant that anything said was interpreted – or misinterpreted – four different ways (unluckily for me, as I was the one who had to sort things out after tempers flared over a syntax error).

Most of our early difficulties were ones of translation, and once we'd worked out what the misunderstanding was, we often found we were actually all saying the same thing.

In general, I'd say that I appear to be a lot less sensitive than I really am. This is largely because my middle-child mentality makes me feel I always have to be the anchor, which means that when everyone else is getting fired up, I try to simmer things down (although, in truth, there are also elements of the drama king in me). The Il Divo guys all have very strong temperaments that can flare up without a moment's notice. I never really believed in the old cliché about explosive Latin temperaments, but I now know that they can be every bit as volatile as people say. Carlos and Sébastien are both given to taking things very personally, and I have also learned just how maddening my PC American tendencies can be for them at times.

I never really believed in the old cliché about explosive Latin temperaments, but I now know that they can be every bit as volatile as people say.

Americans, to our detriment, can seem to be very impersonal, very unfeeling, when we are communicating with others. This usually comes from a desire to be concise, to make ourselves crystal clear, but when we don't engage emotionally with people or express our feelings, it can be mistaken for a kind of haughtiness. When this is the case, we can stir up emotional reactions in other people.

We tumbled into a relationship of 'I love you,' 'I hate you,' 'I'll kill you for sure.' And although at times we got so mad with each other we would be spitting tacks, we also discovered that we could be honest with each other and that our disagreements were not terminal. Whenever there is a bit of tension, I go into my middle-child thing of doing the exact opposite to what everybody else is doing in order to counterbalance things. When we've had a rough couple of days on tour, for example, and everyone is tired and starting to split hairs, I go into clown mode to try to lighten things up. But if the other guys are in a clowning mood, I'll go quiet and introverted. It's always a bad thing to have one clown too many.

Fortunately, we each have a very good sense of humour and we can all play the fool at times. Sébastien and I have a very...somewhat...not-at-all similar sense of humour; Carlos gives me the biggest belly laughs; Urs's humour is layered with Swiss propriety. When he cracks a joke, the timing is so precise, so perfect, that it's absolutely hilarious. He's like one of those clocks that has a cuckoo pop out precisely at the moment the hour strikes.

I must say that after hanging out with the Il Divo guys and using so many different languages to communicate, my grammar has certainly become very interesting. Carlos and Sébastien sometimes mess up their sentences, and even though Urs usually has a better grasp of grammar than most English-speakers, we have got into the habit of using a kind of shorthand – Divospeak. It's easier than forever correcting them. I feel particularly bad for Carlos; he's so caught between the different languages that he has even momentarily forgotten how to speak in Spanish on occasion.

At the very least, though, these kinds of language problems force us to explain ourselves and keep on doing so until we get through. We've learned that many problems can be resolved if we accept that communication is not just about getting your point across; the other person has a point they want to make too. That lesson served me well, and I began to appreciate that what someone says and what someone else hears can be two very different things and that this is often influenced by the individually coloured lenses through which we look at life. So sometimes additional patience is needed.

I can now connect with each of the guys in different ways. There is not one of them whom I don't like as a person or wouldn't have considered being friends with if we'd sat down together in a bar.

I can now connect with each of the guys in different ways. There is not one of them whom I don't like as a person or wouldn't have considered being friends with if we'd sat down together in a bar. It's very interesting how the dynamics work. Put three of us in a room, in any combination, and it's easy. Add the fourth person and there's a teeter-totter imbalance which, although it doesn't always happen, can lead to conflict. Lately it has been so much better, though. Once we started touring, when all the stress of trying to find our sound and get the ball rolling was in the past, all the difficulties began to iron out. It's a close relationship now and getting closer all the time.

Making our first Il Divo album and video required all the professionalism we could muster. We had no time to really get to know each other and get accustomed to each other's styles, and that proved to be a real challenge. We came into the studio, shook hands and said, 'Okay, let's get on with it. Let's get busy and sing our hearts out.' We actually recorded some forty-five tracks, of which only twelve ended up on the first album.

Our combined force outweighs anything we can do on our own, and that when the four of us come together as a united front, the result can be awesome.

Recording that album – and the ones that followed – was about as much fun as getting waxed or having a root canal. We each have a different take on what makes a good song or a good album, so more often than not we don't see eye-to-eye when we start working on a song. Luckily, though, we have a mutual respect for each other and what we each contribute to a song, whether or not we admit it in the heat of the moment. We may disagree, we may even fight about it and want to smack each other upside the head, but the thing we keep in mind is that we all want the same thing: an amazing album.

What we have come to realize is that our combined force outweighs anything we can do on our own, and that when the four of us come together as a united front, the result can be awesome. It's a case of acknowledging that the majority rules, and that's how it needs to work, whatever the issue. It's only when we forget this and become four individuals wanting four different outcomes that nothing gets done.

Those occasions are pretty rare, though. People often say that for a group of male singers we are unusually well behaved, and I think that's cool. If we have missed an interview or a flight or been late for anything, it has always been because of circumstances beyond our control, and we've certainly never trashed a hotel room.

One of the most incredible things to us was how fast music-lovers took to opera singers *not* singing opera. We'd barely hit the shelves with our first album when we were told we were number one in a number of countries. It was very hard to take in. Robbie Williams wasn't too happy when we knocked him off the number-one slot. That was an extraordinary week for us.

MARSHA

Just two days after we heard we were number one, we were walking down the red carpet at the premiere of the movie *Bridget Jones: The Edge of Reason* when Robbie came up to us and said, 'You're the bastards that knocked me off the charts!' We thought he was going to start something right then and there, but he was laughing and congratulated us and we had a photo taken of us together.

I always find it difficult when I'm asked what the 'eureka' moment of my life was because there have been so many. One was the first time I performed the leading role in Gounod's opera of *Romeo and Juliet*. Romeo is one of my all-time favourite roles, both from a dramatic and vocal point of view, and I was thrilled that my family was able to be there to see it. This performance was in Pittsburgh after I had done my apprentice programme there, and they gave me the role as a graduation present. That was very special.

> If I were asked what I enjoy most about being in Il Divo, I'd have to say 'How long have you got?'

Another very special occasion was when my family attended a performance of *La Bohème* on Broadway. Yet another, an Il Divo moment this time, was when we went on the Oprah show for the first time to promote our first album and my family, all bursting with pride, was in the audience. Simon Cowell was on that show, so it was mostly about him, but he brought us on at the very end, saying, 'Here's my group, Il Divo, which I am introducing to America for the first time,' and we sang 'Regresa a Mi'.

Oprah has an aftershow that goes out on a different network and has a question-and-answer format so she can talk to the audience. When she opened up the slot that day, several people in the studio called out, 'Where's Il Divo? Bring them back on!' So she did. We were already getting changed when the message came through: 'Guys, get dressed. They want you back on'. As it was just before Mother's Day, we went back on and sang 'Mama', and, as my mom was right there in the audience, I had to focus real hard to keep it together. That was a special freeze-frame moment for me.

Making our very first video, being invited on the Oprah show twice, going to Japan and making our debut on the same stage where the Beatles had made their debut there – all these things kept hitting us, wave after wave. I pinched myself so often I was black and blue. Performing at the World Cup was fantastic. We were told that we had an audience of over 700 million people, but as we couldn't actually see them, we didn't feel overwhelmed.

If I were asked what I enjoy most about being in Il Divo, I'd have to say 'How long have you got?' I'm spoiled for choice. Travelling to so many foreign lands and being able to experience new and wonderful cultures; having the opportunity to bring my voice and my music to millions of people all over the world; living the life of a rock star – it's impossible to choose between them. There have been so many highlights. There are also sacrifices, though. The hours are gruelling. The jet-lag is never-ending. Sometimes I wake up not knowing where I am, what city I am in. But the hardest thing of all is that time for my girlfriend is so severely limited, and time for family and friends is almost non-existent.

But the highlights make the sacrifices worthwhile. In 2006, I found myself really looking forward to our first world tour. Performing live is what the four of us are cut out to do, what we love doing, what we were used to doing in our solo careers, and it was the one thing we had truly missed throughout those previous two phenomenal Il Divo years.

Each one of us always tries our level best to work to full capacity and give 100 per cent at all times, and I knew the live tour would be no exception, however exhausted we would be by the end of it. And that proved to be the case. We hoped that people would walk away from our shows believing that the two hours they had just spent watching and listening to us were two hours well spent – and they let us know that that was exactly how they felt.

Each one of us always tries our level best to work to full capacity and give one hundred per cent at all times, and I knew the live tour would be no exception, however exhausted we would be by the end of it.

Interviewers are always asking me if I have a favourite venue or location, but the truth is that I don't. Appearing at the Greek Theatre in Los Angeles was an interesting experience, but only in as much as we were putting together our first live DVD and that venue was just great for that. In general, though, I am of the opinion that every performance should be treated the same, no matter what the circumstances, and the presence of cameras certainly shouldn't change how one sings or performs. I try to maintain the same high level of performance wherever we are.

Another question people often ask me is: 'When you sing, do you sing for one person in particular, or do you just pick out one face in the audience?' The answer – perhaps disappointingly – is 'no' on both counts. When I sing, I prefer to sing for lots of people rather than for any one individual.

To be honest, I really love being on what I call a 'proper high-up stage' because it forms a barrier between me and the audience. And one of the reasons I enjoyed my days in opera so much was because I had a character to play in which I could lose myself and an orchestra down below in the pit adding even more distance between me and the people I was performing for.

When I'm standing alongside the other guys in Il Divo, however, it's just David. Of course there's the orchestra – or a band – and we are in suits, which are a kind of costume, but it's still just David. People are not looking at a character, they are looking at me. They think they know me, but they don't. They know my voice, know me from interviews and the Il Divo videos, but they don't know the real me. I like that because it means I get to keep a piece of myself for myself.

I wouldn't trade in what I'm doing now for anything. So much of what has happened has exceeded our hopes and expectations, and the future seems wide open.

Life is full of crazy contradictions. For example, I've never suffered from stage-fright, but I sure do suffer from *after*-stage-fright. I absolutely adore being on stage and being an exhibitionist, but when people come to the stage door after a show or wait for us on the sidewalk, I become a bit of an introvert again, like when I was a kid, and I don't know how to deal with it. That's the after-stage-fright.

I wouldn't trade in what I'm doing now for anything. So much of what has happened has exceeded our hopes and expectations, and the future seems wide open. But we still have to keep ourselves grounded in the music, in our passion for the music and for performing. We've been given an opportunity like no other: the chance to bring a new style of music into the world. That kind of chance only comes once in a lifetime, and when it does you have to grab hold of it with both hands and enjoy the journey. At the same time, we are not superhuman, not just mannequins dressed by Armani. We're regular guys who, as long as we can keep on reinventing ourselves and continue to enjoy what life throws at us, will have a brilliant future.

Our travels around the world have brought us into contact with so many different cultures. Every time we go to Japan, I have such a fascinating time. I have a real affinity for the Japanese culture. Even as far back as fourth grade, when our class was studying cultures of the world, I remember the unit on Japan stood out from the others, and I always planned to take a trip there. From what I understand, it is a very difficult market to break into, so it is a real honour that they have not only warmed to us, but have truly embraced us and enjoy our music.

Our first promotional trip to Japan was great fun because, as I have mentioned, we performed a showcase set on the stage where the Beatles debuted in the sixties. But it was our return, almost a year later, for our live show that proved beyond a shadow of a doubt that our music has no culture or language barriers.

At the arrivals hall of Tokyo's Narita Airport we were greeted by thousands of fans and several news crews. We were stunned. Flashbulbs were going off all over the place, fans were screaming and reaching out to us and store-bought and homemade Il Divo posters, T-shirts and hats were everywhere. Well over thirty police and airport security had to usher us through the terminal or it would have turned into pandemonium. If we didn't feel like rock stars before, we surely did after that!

> Our fans remind us how the word 'fan' comes from 'fanatic' – and we love them for it . . . Their ages range from thirteen to eighty-five, and they certainly aren't all women.

Our fans remind us how the word 'fan' comes from 'fanatic' – and we love them for it. Initially, it was believed that Il Divo's fanbase would be of a certain type: housewives. As we started taking our music around the world, however, we saw how diverse our fans are. Their ages range from thirteen to eighty-five, and they certainly aren't all women. We welcome them all. Without our fans, we wouldn't have a reason to make music. We set up a website for them to communicate on and they have created communities of people that have us as their common thread. That's a nice thing. Given that we live in a world where there is so much suffering, it's great to be at the centre of a community that is so heart-warming and has so much goodwill.

Three years ago, while we were having a brainstorming session about the content for our website, we came up with the idea of making videos. No one had any idea how to do this, so I volunteered to start getting some footage together for possible use.

I started by using my iSight camera hooked into my computer. I would carry my laptop around with me and shove it in the guys' faces. At first they didn't mind, and I was having fun learning a lot about iMovie and the movie-making process. But carrying the computer around became tedious after the first video was done during our first promo trip around Europe, so I invested in a nice little handheld camera, which took digital video. The quality wasn't that great, but it was a lot easier than porting around a computer. By the third video, I realized that I had a true passion for making movies. Every aspect is intriguing to me.

The boys have started calling me Cecil B. DeMiller, because I do everything from footage to editing to sound design, and so on. The page on our website that houses my videos has been getting around a million requests a week from fans around the world. It's been an amazing response to what was merely a frivolity. I'm just glad that the public appreciates the hours I put in and doesn't dismiss it as bad YouTube fodder.

Since then, almost on a daily basis, I still have to pinch myself to believe that this is really happening. There is one high after another. The other guys and I have shared so many amazing experiences. It's all so new to us, we have to make light of it, almost as a buffer against how excited we are. If we really let out how we feel all the time, we'd be like nerdy little boys. When we first started, it was an experiment that could have fizzled out overnight, so every success we have had has confirmed that we are doing a good job, that the music we've put out there is being well received. Doors keep opening for us and we keep walking right through them.

Since then, almost on a daily basis, I still have to pinch myself to believe that this is really happening. There is one high after another.

I always find it difficult to say what my favourite Il Divo song is. In truth, I don't really have a favourite. What I enjoy about what we do is the public's reaction. Each song has something special that people react to in different ways, and seeing that happen song after song is what thrills me about performing live. In terms of an actual brilliant musical piece, though, I think I'd choose 'Somewhere' by that genius Leonard Bernstein. Sometimes when we are singing that song, I think of my parents and how they hauled me and my sisters out of San Diego and set off for Colorado with only their faith – the faith to believe that somewhere there *was* a place for us – and the strength to keep going until we found it. And when that happens, it gives me the strength to continue doing whatever needs to be done to keep the music alive. And, if sharing that doesn't prove that I'm an American who's learned how to engage with his feelings, I don't know what will!

Sébastien

Je Ne Regrette Rien

We did not have a lot of money when I was a child and there was even one occasion when I was driven to steal food. Not surprisingly, perhaps, when I mentioned this recently to a newspaper reporter, the title that was emblazoned on top of the interview was 'Il Thievo'. As it was such a clever play on words, I didn't mind. My present-day life, though, and my hopes for the future, are still influenced by the tough times I experienced as a child, and I now know that those days will never be erased completely from my memory. Rough times leave a scar, but they also make you stronger, and it is because of my scars that I am the person I am today.

Until I was six, all was well in my world. I lived with my mother, Marie, and my father in a tiny 10-metre square room that was once the servants' quarters of a very large building in the Sixteenth Arrondissement, a very chic, exclusive residential area of Paris, where there are many opulent privately owned mansions and embassies. It is a very expensive area, famous for its Quartier Chaillot, its grand Second Empire avenues, elegant cafés, fascinating museums and the Jardins du Trocadéro. The building we lived in was owned by my maternal great-grandmother, Mémé Denise. It was given to her as a wedding gift in the 1870s and many other family members also lived there.

The good times, though, were not to last. Soon after my sixth birthday, my father abandoned my mother and me and left home, never to return. While he was there we had very little money, but now we had less. Our world was turned upside down.

Although my mother, who worked in clothing stores and since 1980 as a fashion stylist, always managed to put some food on our plates, it was very basic and she had a really hard time doing so, though she did well in giving us a balanced diet. On one occasion, after she'd mentioned that she would dearly love to have a melon but I knew we couldn't afford it, I went to an expensive *épicerie* just outside our building, picked one up, tucked it inside my jacket and legged it. I knew I was doing wrong, but the desire to please her far outweighed any fear of being caught.

Soon after my sixth birthday, my father abandoned my mother and me and left home, never to return. While he was there we had very little money, but now we had less.

When I got home with my trophy, however, things did not work out quite as I had expected. Far from thanking me, my mum was absolutely horrified by what I had done and, having given me a lengthy talking-to about stealing, she marched me straight back to the *épicerie* and made me give it back to the person in charge. She was right to do this, of course, and it was such an awful, humiliating experience that it cured me of shoplifting forever, there and then.

It was not the end of my juvenile delinquency, however. For example, when I was about ten, I stole a cheque from my uncle's bureau after he had refused to buy me a toy when we were out together shopping. Back at my great-grandmother Mémé Denise's country house, where he lived, I sneaked into his room, opened the bureau drawer and tore a cheque from his cheque book. I'd seen him do that when paying for things and I thought that was all that was necessary. When I went back to the shop to buy the toy, the assistant took one look at the blank cheque, picked up the phone and rang my uncle.

'Your nephew is here with an unsigned cheque,' I heard her say, and, as I shifted from one foot to the other, I knew then that I had been a *really* bad boy and I was in for it.

Uncle Pierre, who was actually my maternal grandmother's brother and a lovely man really, was so angry when I returned to the house that he slapped me very hard and made me cry. I was so furious about this that I took my revenge at the first opportunity. I crept into his bedroom, dragged some of his suits out of the wardrobe and sat there making little cuts in them with a pair of nail scissors. The next time my uncle put on one of the jackets, he saw immediately what I had done and burst into my great-grandmother's room to show her. Once she was over the initial shock, though, Mémé Denise just tossed back her head and laughed, adding, 'I'm glad. They were ugly suits and you need to buy new ones anyway.' That made him even more furious. I'm pretty sure her attitude was 'Serves you right. You shouldn't have been so mean and should have bought him the toy. You have a lot of money and he doesn't.'

As my mother always had to work such long hours to support us, I got used to being a latchkey kid and home alone, and I soon learned to be independent. By the time I was twelve I was baking cakes as a treat for her when she came home from work late at night.

As my mother always had to work such long hours to support us, I got used to being a latchkey kid and home alone, and I soon learned to be independent. By the time I was twelve I was baking cakes as a treat for her when she came home.

One way or another, it was not an easy childhood, and because I still find it very painful to remember certain things, it remains a subject I do not like talking about to anyone. For me, growing up was more a case of growing out of trouble. Before the age of six, I witnessed a lot of violence, drugs and bad behaviour, the kind of stuff that nobody, least of all a kid, should see. Witnessing such things has an impact on your psyche, makes you very wary and introverted and inclined to bottle things up and keep everything to yourself, but thanks to the specialist help that children can get I think I've been able to deal with my troubled childhood.

After my father left, my mother, who was only eighteen when she had me, never really had a life of her own and I've never forgotten the sacrifices she made for me while I was growing up. As soon as I made any real money, which I did when I joined Il Divo, my first thought was to help her financially and pay off all her debts. I also bought her a kitten, which she loves. It made me feel really happy to be able to do things like that for her.

Throughout my childhood, I used to stay with my *grand-mère* Jacqueline a great deal. I was forever traipsing back and forth between her flat, which was on the second floor, and my mum's room at the top of the building. My 'Mimine' was always, and still is, a key figure in my life, and she, as well as my mother, was chiefly responsible for making me the person I am today. Although '*mamie*' is a word used for 'grandmother' in French, I never liked it because it made her seem older than she was – she was only twenty when she had my mother. Instead, I used to call her 'Mimine' – which means 'little hand' in French – because she was so gentle and used to stroke my forehead and pat my cheeks with her hand. She had a bit of money, but my mother was always very proud and independent and would not accept any help from anybody, including her mother.

My 'Mimine' was always, and still is, a key figure in my life

Most of the time while I was growing up, I lived in my imagination, in my own world, where life was colourful rather than black and white. I was like a sponge, absorbing everything, keeping everything inside. Unusually for a kid, I often dreamed of owning a house, and I knew exactly what kind of house it would be. To me a home symbolised shelter and protection for the people I loved and would love. When I was out and about, I would stand gazing at various houses and if they were particularly attractive, I would go off into a reverie and think, 'Yes, that would do. I'd like to live in that one.' Now, thanks to Il Divo, I've achieved that childhood ambition. I now own two homes, one in London where I spend most of my time and one in Paris, for holidays. It means I will always be able to provide shelter for my family and friends, should they need it.

My childhood was often quite confusing. Mémé Denise owned a very nice country house, about forty-five minutes from Paris in Louveciennes, and my life was comfortable when I stayed there. I could eat gourmet food to my heart's content: there were always mouth-watering *petit-fours* and other little specialities on the side tables. I loved the simple things of being there, listening to the birds, picking blueberries to make delicious blueberry tarts, going to church on Sundays with Mémé Denise, feeling the grass between my toes and just being with family. Christmas was just wonderful there. The house was always beautiful, but even more so during the festivities. Above all, it was a time when everybody in the family was together, a time when I felt secure and loved, a time that allowed me to forget the struggles and hardship of the other eleven months of the year. Christmas is still my favourite time of year. I love decorating the tree and cooking a meal for the people I love.

Another confusion was that because I came from the Sixteenth Arrondissement and went to school with boys who mostly came from wealthy backgrounds, people always assumed I must be a rich kid too. The truth was that, despite working very hard, my mum never made much money. I did, however, find a group of friends whose backgrounds were not dissimilar to mine. I never really minded being different from the other boys at school, because I always succeeded in making friends, regardless of my social position or theirs. To this day, I respect people whatever their situation in life. It's second nature for me to thank the man who drives the limousines we travel around in or the porter who collects my bags.

'I love that about you,' Renée, my fiancée, is always saying. 'Not everybody does that.' She is the same way: she respects people, no matter who they are or what they do.

I guess the fact that I didn't have an entirely comfortable childhood has made me more sensitive and more likely to sympathise with other people's problems. Three years ago I met Dr Philippe who introduced me to *Assistance Médicale Toit du Monde* (AMTM), a really inspiring charity that helps impoverished communities gain access to clean water and medical care, among other vital assistance. All the money donated goes straight to the people in need, so Il Divo and I now support it in whatever way we can. It makes me very happy to be able to do that. Now that I'm so often away with Il Divo, I am no longer able to go into hospitals like I used to now and then and play the guitar for kids who have cancer and other life-threatening conditions, but I carry them in my heart all the time.

I guess the fact that I didn't have an entirely comfortable childhood has made me more sensitive and more likely to sympathise with other people's problems.

These days, compared to many people, I am well off, but because the influences of my past experiences linger on, I don't feel secure, and I definitely still have my feet planted firmly on the ground. For example, although I enjoy flying around on private jets, being chauffeured everywhere and staying in luxury hotels, I also love spending a couple of weeks every year at a friend Nollane's house in the south of France, which is literally falling down around his ears. When I'm there, I sleep on a mattress on the floor, wash dishes, cook meals and shower outdoors. I'm able to bathe my senses in listening to the ocean, smelling fresh lavender and pine trees, and that brings me back to reality. I need to do this sometimes, it's always been those simple things that I cherish.

My early experiences have left me with three legacies. They have made me very cautious about how I use money, left me wanting to care for the people I love and to give to those who are less fortunate than myself. Over the years, I have heard so many scary stories about artists blowing all the money they have earned and then going bust because they could not pay their taxes, and I am determined that will not happen to me.

My early experiences have left me with three legacies. They have made me very cautious about how I use money, left me wanting to care for the people I love and to give to those who are less fortunate than myself.

I have remained very close to my mother, but I have found it difficult to forget all the things that happened to me as a kid. I realize she was suffering from stress caused by some bad life experiences and I don't doubt that I was a difficult child at times, but I think she took things out on me in a way that maybe she shouldn't have. One period I've never forgotten is when she had an accident and I had to stay at my Mémé Denise's house in the country for a month with my grandmother Mimine. When I returned home, my mother was still hobbling about on crutches, which she used to brandish at me. Then when I was seventeen I decided that I couldn't tolerate being the victim of my mother's rages any more. I grabbed her and said, 'Never do that again. *Jamais, jamais*.' Later that day I left home and went to live with my grandmother, and my mother and I remained estranged for some time. Now that we are close again, she really is helpful and a good mother. She's very proud of what I am doing, especially when her friends say, 'So your son is one of the singers in Il Divo.' I think that makes her happy.

The occasion I remember most clearly from my adolescence is when I was playing the piano in my grandmother's flat. Mimine, who had been quite ill and in a coma for a brief while, claimed she was now having premonitions and visions. That day, she came into the room while I was playing, paused by me and said, 'Do you know what, Sébastien? You are going to be a composer one day and will definitely have a career in music.'

'No, no, Mimine,' I muttered, 'I'm going to be a pilot.'

'There's no money in composing,' my mother Marie exclaimed. 'He's going to be a banker. That's where the money is.' She used to dress artists and knew what a hard business it was; she wanted a financially secure life for me and not one similar to my childhood.

I noticed, though, that there was a rather desperate expression on my mother's face as she said this. She was only too aware that I wasn't great at knuckling down to my studies.

In those days people were always telling me I was hopeless and a bad student and that I would never amount to anything. Surprisingly, these criticisms didn't make me feel downhearted. On the contrary, they made me all the more determined to prove otherwise. Later on, when I realized my eyesight was too poor for me to be a pilot for a big company like Air France, I was upset, but tried to be philosophical. 'Okay,' I thought, 'that dream's over. But I have an even greater passion in my life: music. If I work really hard at it, all will be well.' I worked so hard, in fact, that it became my whole life, so much so that I sometimes forgot to eat; the music became my food, my energy. I would sit there, eyes closed, dreaming of nothing but music for hours and hours. It became my everything, and it still is today. I've always thought that dreams are very important. People who find themselves stuck in a rut are in that position because they have no dreams. You have to have dreams. If you don't, you can't make them come true. I once read somewhere, '*Vie tes reves, mais ne reve pas ta vie.*' I love the meaning of this – Live your dreams, but don't dream your life.

In those days people were always telling me I was hopeless and a bad student and that I would never amount to anything. Surprisingly, these criticisms didn't make me feel downhearted. On the contrary, they made me all the more determined to prove otherwise.

So making music, whether on the piano, the guitar, or later through my voice, has always been a passion and a refuge for me. I also love listening to music. It always tugs at my heartstrings and has the power to transform my moods and evoke a whole range of emotions. Music is heaven's gift to humanity. It intoxicates, consoles, reconciles and inspires, and takes us to previously uncharted emotional territory. I know of no better tonic in life; it's a perfect way to dissolve the blues and raise the spirits.

My feelings for music are so strong that I honestly feel, without wishing to sound melodramatic, that I couldn't go on living without it. Perhaps this stems from the fact that I was an only child and often lonely when I was growing up. I used to listen to music all the time; even when I was trying to get to sleep, I had to have the radio on. For me, music was a therapy, a refuge, an escape from the harsh realities of life, and I have always relied on it to get me through the darkest of moments.

Given that it has always been so important to me, it's perhaps not surprising that some of my most cherished early memories are to do with music. One of my ambitions, which I hope to realize in the not too distant future, is to meet David Bowie. His was the first concert I was ever taken to, when I was just four years old, and my admiration for him started there.

That was the moment I realized that what I wanted most in life was to be a composer and a musician, and, despite my mother's desire to see me become a banker, I followed my own dream

The breakthrough moment came when I was about eight and staying with my Mémé Denise, who was still quite wealthy in those days. On this occasion, there was a black-and-white movie on the television, which I was thoroughly enjoying watching, but the accompanying piano music was really dreadful and doing absolutely nothing for the moment of high romance being played out on the screen. Having listened for a bit, I crossed over to the TV, turned down the volume, then went to my grandma's piano and started composing some music to accompany the film.

That was the moment I realized that what I wanted most in life was to be a composer and a musician, and, despite my mother's desire to see me become a banker, I followed my own dream and forged a career as a singer/songwriter. I was so lucky to have had a moment like that at such a young age. Some people wait a lifetime for such a revelation. For me, it was an out-of-the-blue moment that determined the direction my life would take. I've always thought that music is a gift that we receive at birth and thereafter it is a matter of listening and responding and making that inner voice heard.

When I was growing up my mum had a boyfriend for ten years, Mathieu. He was a British musician and composer who spent a lot of time listening to the Beatles and classical music. That is where my love of the Beatles began – and I have listened to them ever since. My favourite Beatle is John Lennon; nobody could begin to imagine how much I would have loved to meet him.

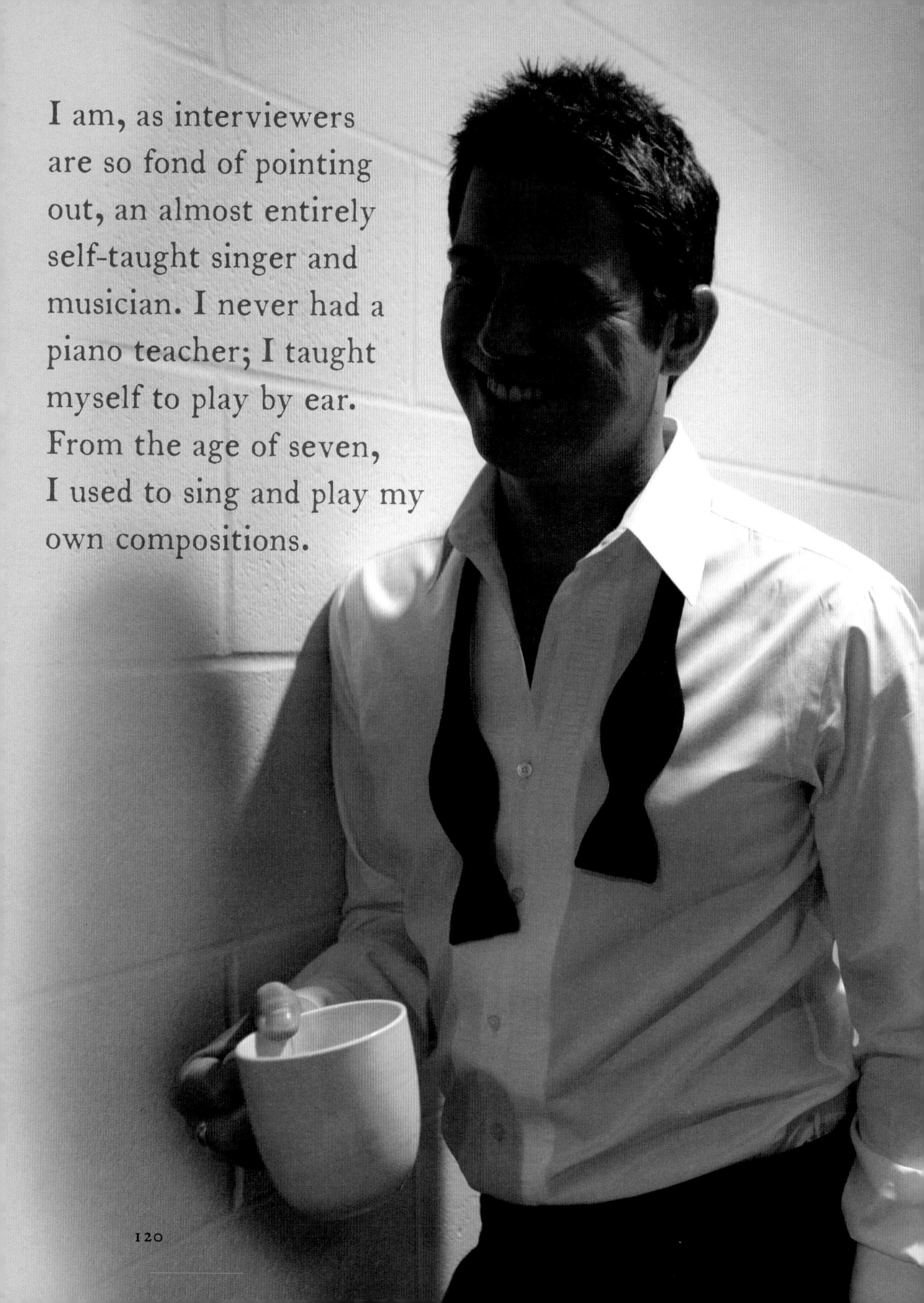

I am, as interviewers are so fond of pointing out, an almost entirely self-taught singer and musician. I never had a piano teacher; I taught myself to play by ear. From the age of seven, I used to sing and play my own compositions.

If I ever find myself shipwrecked on a desert island, I hope I will have the Beatles' *White Album* with me, along with David Bowie's *The Rise and Fall of Ziggy Stardust and the Spiders From Mars*, Chris de Burgh's 'The Lady in Red', Jeff Buckley's second album *Grace* and albums by some of my other favourite artists: Coldplay, Sting, Garbage, Supertramp, The The, ZZ Top, Frank Sinatra – and many more, if I could carry them (am I allowed to take a huge suitcase, please?).

I'd also like to have some of my favourite Il Divo songs with me. My favourite is 'Every Time I Look At You', which we included on our first album. It is such a gentle, romantic song and I'm really attached to it. I love the words and the melody and I think the harmonies are very subtle. I also have a soft spot for 'My Way', which is on the same album, because I think it was very daring of us to sing a song that many of the major singers in the world have tackled at one time or another. I also love 'La Vida Sin Amor', which is a new song on our latest album, *Siempre*. The melody is very upbeat Latino, which is a new direction for us, and I'm so glad we recorded it. It's always a big hit when we perform it live, and one I can't help but dance to! 'Regresa a Mi', the song we sang together as Il Divo for the first time, will always be a favourite too, for sentimental reasons.

I am, as interviewers are so fond of pointing out, an almost entirely self-taught singer and musician. I never had a piano teacher; I taught myself to play by ear. From the age of seven, I used to sing and play my own compositions. At such times I thought I was Mozart! I was always inspired by classical music, which my mother's boyfriend Mathieu used to listen to on the radio, and I loved trying to play some of the classical arias (but you wouldn't have recognised them they were so bad). Later, when I was about twelve, I took up the guitar. I had lessons for about six months. When it comes to reading music, I learned the basic notation for the guitar, but most of the time I still play both the guitar and piano – and compose – by ear.

I was never in a choir, but I do remember going to church at Christmas with my grandfather Papy Paul and I loved singing the hymns at full volume. My grandfather, however, was not at all happy about this and would nudge me and tell me off for being too loud. He was obviously embarrassed, thought I was making a fool of myself, but my passion for singing was always there, right from the beginning, and nobody could put me down for long. From about the age of fourteen, I used to sing in the Paris subway with my friend Hélène and a bunch of others, just to experience the feeling of being a performer and having a crowd watch us. Hélène was a soprano in the French National Radio Chorus and went to the Radio France music school. We would meet up in the metro on the way to school. She was my first childhood love, but I was too shy to do anything about it at the time. Now she is married to a lovely man, expecting their first child, and we are still great friends.

Later on, I had two singing lessons, but I didn't enjoy either of them and never went again. I was convinced the tutor was trying to erase all the emotion from my voice and I really didn't like that. I thought it was like being at school, where there was no freedom. I only realise now that I needed the tools and technique that the tutor was trying to teach me.

When I was seventeen, I used to go out on boat trips on the Seine for my friends' birthday parties and while on board I would play my guitar, for the sheer love of it. A little later, I played piano (very badly) in several Parisian bars and helped out with the karaoke. I got paid for those gigs and really loved doing them. I also remember going to Sweden with my cousin Gregory as he was a big fan of horses and the French were in Sweden for the showjumping world championship. I won't lie, like most teenage boys we also went to discover Swedish girls! We ran out of money while we were there and I had no choice but to busk. Fortunately, Swedish people love music and were very kind to me. It was when I was twenty that my then-girlfriend Diane encouraged me to take my singing much more seriously and concentrate on that, rather than the piano or guitar.

I was not always lucky with my early singing moments. When I was still a teenager – and passionately in love – I once played my guitar and sang a song I had composed for the girl with whom I was in love. This was in Saint-Germain-des-Prés, at midnight, on 21 June which is the *Fête de la Musique*, the day the French celebrate music. A local neighbour was not appreciative of my efforts and came to his window shouting, '*Tais-toi* (shut up)! *Va-t'en* (clear off)!' When I persisted, he flung a bucket of water over my head and I was left standing there drenched to the skin. My best friend Benji, who was with me, was laughing so hard.

Soon after that, events took a more promising turn, and after having made several demo records which featured my own compositions and many bitterly disappointing visits to record companies, I had a really lucky break. I got my first recording contract with EMI and my solo album *Libre* was released in June 2000. I was so thrilled when I read that, thanks to this album, I'd been dubbed 'the new prodigy of French pop' by one music critic. Praise indeed! The album included 'Je t'en Veux' ('I'm Mad at You'), a song I composed when I was about sixteen years old, and 'Libre' ('Freedom'), which made it into the French charts.

When I worked on *Libre*, I arranged the songs with another guy, Lionel Tridon. That's something I love doing. Lionel is a very talented French arranger and drummer who became a very special person to me – very important and inspirational. I learned so much from him over the three years of making songs together at his studio in Replonge near Lognes, 40 kilometres north of Paris. He helped me create a fabulous album, and he and his entire family have always been so supportive of me. During those days, I also started to arrange music for other people and became recognized a little bit as a songwriter, something that came about when my publisher put me in touch with other musicians and singers. I have just succeeded in buying back the rights for *Libre*, and I've re-released it online.

Being signed up by EMI (thank you Mr Frederique Juarez) and recording *Libre* at the age of twenty-three remains one of the most exciting events of my life. Jean-Pierre Janiaud, who works with so many French stars, people I really admire, was the sound engineer on that album and so important to the whole project. The process of being in a recording studio was so exciting, I really didn't mind working from morning till night. I was only too happy to work my fingers to the bone. Perhaps because I was the one who had to make all the decisions, I found the whole business of promoting my first album much less glamorous than making it. That is not a concern these days, though, because in Il Divo there are four of us making the decisions and sharing the promotional work.

The process of being in a recording studio was so exciting, I really didn't mind working from morning till night.

In 2002, I had another lucky break. I was offered the two plum roles of the Grande Personne and the Businessman in Richard Cocciante's musical production of *Le Petit Prince*. This job came about when my uncle, Gerard, who had connections in the music world, heard that the producers were casting. He made a telephone call to a friend on my behalf and I was invited to go along for an audition. The person who was really instrumental in me getting those parts, however, was the writer Elizabeth Anais, who penned the lyrics.

Le Petit Prince was a wonderful musical, based on Saint-Exupéry's famous novel of the same title. As it was to be my first and last musical before joining Il Divo, I was incredibly fortunate to be in a show that had such a good story and beautiful music and that ran for eight months at the Casino de Paris.

I had two costume-changes for that production, one for my role as the Grande Personne, who wants to be admired by everyone and lives alone on a planet so he cannot hear anything uncomplimentary said about him, and one for my role as the Businessman, who is constantly busy counting the stars, which he thinks he owns. When playing the latter, I had to be suspended high above the stage, which was a big problem for me as I suffer from vertigo. Once up there, the only way I could find my voice and sing was to stay put on a specially constructed platform. I felt terrible throughout, but as I didn't want to lose the job, I just had to grin and bear it and get used to feeling giddy and nauseous.

The stage director for that production was Jean-Louis Martinoti, who came from the world of opera. What a gifted man! Such a perfectionist. I learned something new from him every day. I really couldn't have wished for a better person to guide me in my first musical. He was so kind and generous, eccentric, funny, yet so honest. The team spirit he created on *Le Petit Prince* was absolutely amazing and, as a result, some of my closest friends stem from that time, friends who I still see whenever I am in Paris. Whenever we meet, we all agree that our time in *Le Petit Prince* was magical, and it's certainly a period I look back on with tremendous affection.

As well as special times like that, I did have quite a few horrible times. The business I am in is renowned for being very up-and-down, and all I can say is that the bad times really do make you appreciate the good times. Just before Il Divo came along, I was going through a very difficult patch. With no work on the horizon after *Le Petit Prince,* I was almost on the breadline and didn't have sufficient money left to pay the mortgage on my flat, even though I was working hard at the time on my second solo album. Just as I was starting to panic, the audition for Il Divo cropped up. My life in those days was rather like that: every time I was close to the edge, something happened to get me out of trouble. As a result, I do believe in Lady Luck, but I also know that if we are to fulfil our destinies, we have to make things happen.

The business I am in is renowned for being very up-and-down, and all I can say is that the bad times really do make you appreciate the good times. Just before Il Divo came along, I was going through a very difficult patch.

The man who totally altered the course of my life and brought me to where I am today was Simon Cowell. He is the one who deserves all the credit for bringing Il Divo into being. He had the vision and he never faltered, even though it took so many agents two years to sift through singers from seventeen countries before they found the four of us.

My audition for Il Divo actually came about when I went for another audition for a musical called *The Sun King*. That turned out to be one of life's extraordinary coincidences. While I was waiting for *The Sun King* audition, I met Geraldine, who is now Carlos's wife, quite by chance through the casting director Bruno, and she told me about the other audition and said

she thought it would be worth a try. Carlos and Geraldine both convinced me to give it a go. I remember Carlos asking me to sing over the internet and saying, 'Wow! You're not too bad.' Thanks, Carlos.

So I went along to audition at La Bastille in Paris, in front of Simon's right-hand man, Sonny Takhar, who has been a guiding light and is responsible for helping me become a member of Il Divo. I sang 'Caruso', one of the songs that we included on *Siempre* and one which I really pushed to have on that album. I had no hopes whatsoever of it going down well at the audition, however. The pianist who was supposed to accompany me that day was absolutely terrible, so I played the piano myself and possibly did an even worse job. 'Okay, that's that,' I thought and, convinced it would lead to nothing, I went into a totally relaxed, couldn't-care-less mode. Nobody could have been more astonished than I when I was asked to meet Simon Cowell. To be honest, I can still hardly believe that I am where I am now: part of an operatic group that has had so much success.

When I went to meet Simon, I didn't have a clue who he was. It didn't take me long to discover, however, that he has in very great measure what the English call 'the gift of the gab'. He really is a very good talker, has this incredible ability to inspire great confidence and make you believe everything he says. He's also, despite his reputation, a very nice person. I *really* like him, and I find him a pleasure to work and socialise with, even when we disagree about things.

When I was offered the job, my manager at the time said, 'Don't do it, Sébastien. Your second album is going to do so well. You are really going places. This is not the moment to change tracks and lose all your contacts in France.'

It was, of course, a big decision to make. I realized from the start that it would involve huge life changes, that I would have to give up most of the time I spent with my family and friends. But having made the decision, helped by my girlfriend at the time, Catherine, a key person in my life, it was a case of *je ne regrette rien*. I remember during the first week in London, calling my manager and Catherine and telling them I couldn't be so far away from my loved ones. Catherine came straight to London. She was a really fantastic support and encouraged me to stay. I have always believed that *all* the experiences we have bring us to where we are today. Of course, I often thought in the past that I would have loved to have had a happier childhood, but I also felt that if I had, I wouldn't be the person I am now. So I always came back to *je ne regrette rien*.

I realized from the start that it would involve huge life changes, that I would have to give up most of the time I spent with my family and friends.

Interestingly, I was to sign my Il Divo contract on the 7th of the month, which confirmed to me that I had made the right decision. The number seven has always been my lucky number. I was born on 7 March 1973, so my birth date is 7373; I began the musical *The Little Prince* on the 7th; then, after signing my Il Divo contract, I found the first house I ever bought on the 7th.

People often ask us if Simon is still involved with the group on a daily basis. The fact is that Simon is a *very* busy man, and these days we meet him on average about once a year, in the springtime, when we are deciding on the repertoire for our next album, although he does supervise things from afar. He took the initiative to start us up and opened a lot of doors for us, but since we released the first album and it was so successful all over the world, it is basically Carlos, David, Urs and I who take care of things now, supported enormously, of course, by SYCO, Sony BMG and our management team.

Peter Rudge, our manager, is a very key figure, and I knew from the moment I first met him that he was the kind of management guy we needed. He has brought so many good things to the table, including the Barbra Streisand tour. He's very good at what he does and I like him a lot. He's like a father-figure to me.

Meredith Plant, his right-hand woman, is amazing too. She's so organized and is absolutely brilliant when we are on the road. She's a girl who's going places; she'll be a terrific manager one day. Gary Casson is a very important member from our management team. He looks after our finances and is a fantastic advisor. All the people, in fact, who work on Il Divo contribute to its success. It's not just us four guys, it's the amazing band, the hard-working crew, our caterers, the sound engineers, our hair and make-up artist Tania, Felicity our stylist, our tour managers Steve and Frankie. The entire team all make Il Divo so successful.

> At first, I thought Il Divo was just going to be another boy-band, but the music we made together soon convinced me that it was going to be much more than that. When I heard 'Feelings', one of the first songs we considered for our first album, it made all the hairs stand up on the back of my neck.

At first, I thought Il Divo was just going to be another boy-band, but the music we made together soon convinced me that it was going to be much more than that. When I heard 'Feelings', one of the first songs we considered for our first album, I thought it was amazing. It made all the hairs stand up on the back of my neck.

Although I understand why some people in the industry think the group is 'manufactured', they're totally missing the point of what Il Divo is all about. The other three guys, who are all classically trained opera singers, will tell you that it's actually very common in the opera world to put people together who have never met before. So, what's the difference?

We're one pop singer and three opera singers, different to any other group before us. And because we all shared the same dream to bring good music to as many people as possible, we were happy to fuse the two musical styles together. The rest, as people are fond of saying, is history. *Vive la difference!*

A number of interviewers have suggested that Carlos, David, Urs and I are like brothers, but that is not how I think of us. I feel our relationship is more like that of an arranged marriage in that we are all determined, whatever problems arise, to make it work. Some days I get along better with one than I do another. Sometimes I have an 'off' day when they are having an 'on' day, and vice versa. I love them all, though.

Of course, tensions arise between us, particularly when we are on the road, and some days can be quite difficult when we have had little sleep, no days off, are missing our families and loved ones, and our own beds. We are all temperamental in our own way, and it's only natural that we need to get away from each other sometimes, especially if we've been spending seventeen hours a day in each other's pockets. However, that is not always how it is. When we were in Sydney, for example, the four of us chose to go to the beach and hang out together, though it was impossible to relax there because there were so many beautiful women floating around.

Something that has surprised – and pleased – me is that all four of us guys have wide musical tastes. Carlos, David and Urs, for example, are not only into classical music and operatic arias. David likes techno, Urs listens to heavy metal, Carlos is a fan of Tom Jones and I am into Radiohead, Coldplay and Muse.

Of course, tensions arise between us, particularly when we are on the road, and some days can be quite difficult. When we have had little sleep, no days off, are missing our families and loved ones, and our own beds.

When asked to describe the other members of the group, I usually say that David is the crazy one, always joking and larking around; Carlos is a volcano, very Spanish, and always says exactly what he thinks; and Urs is quiet, a guy who likes everything to be on time and neatly tied up. As for me, they say I am very French, very sensitive, a person who reacts to the smallest thing. It's true that if, for example, the food is too spicy in a restaurant, I'll let everybody know.

The good news, though, is that we all came into Il Divo with between ten and fifteen years' experience, and even Simon has publicly stated that he sometimes feels intimidated by and slightly in awe of our abilities. We all get involved in what songs should be on our albums. It's a team effort, and Simon, Sonny, Peter Rudge and the rest of our management team trust us. I am very proud of what we do. We knew from the start that we were going do something very different, but none of us had any idea of how well our voices would fuse. What amazes me the most is how diverse our fan base is. People of all ages come to our shows – from kids to grandmothers. It's the kind of mix that most performers dream of, and something that we have achieved.

I love meeting people from different cultures, and I find it incredible that people in places where we have never been know who we are. I now know for sure that music is a universal language. It's all about giving your best to people, touching their hearts and allowing them to renew contact with their own feelings and be unashamedly emotional. We are blessed to have so many loyal fans. The vision I had of the world before I joined Il Divo was very French, very narrow, and now my perception is completely different. My travels have made me more at ease with and more open to others, and I am far less judgmental.

I must say that the throwing of knickers on to the stage is not something I care for, although I do find it funny sometimes. I was not amused, however, when someone threw a pair that hit me right in the eye just as I was about to sing the first line of a song. I felt like a bear in a cage in a zoo. These days, getting pelted with knickers and other intimate items has become part of the job, and one occasion that I remember with a bit of a shudder is when we were in a car, signing autographs after a TV appearance, and a girl passed me something through the window, saying, 'I always think about you when I have it on.' I didn't realize what it was until it started to move and buzz. It was a vibrator! Things like that certainly make life more entertaining.

I do appreciate the wonderful presents we get from our fans, though. The effort that is put into some of these is so touching, even more so because I know not all of them are financially well off.

Performing live is our *raison d'être*, the reason why we all wanted to be singers in the first place, so our two Il Divo tours were a dream come true for all of us. It's marvellous to have the opportunity to visit so many countries around the world, and such a plus to discover that we are successful in so many of the places we visit. On top of this, we are also able to use our fame to do some good in the world, help those who are not as fortunate as ourselves. That is truly the *cerise sur le gateau.*

Life in Il Divo is hectic. We don't actually get any time off; we just try to get some rest when we are travelling, which is usually impossible. It's exhausting at times, although our fans make it all worthwhile and once I'm on that stage I forget all about it. My bed these days is more often than not a seat on an aeroplane and my wardrobe is a suitcase. There is another more serious downside to all the touring we do. I don't want to sound too morbid, but I've always had an inordinate fear of death, and all the take-offs and landings and limousine journeys have not done much to help this. What scares me is the thought of death, of nothing. The very idea of my body becoming dust or ashes is very disturbing to me. I love life and there is still so much I want to experience. I feel that particularly strongly these days. The fact that I've been so blessed makes me even more fearful of it all being taken away.

Life in Il Divo is hectic. We don't actually get any time off; we just try to get some rest when we are travelling, which is usually impossible.

I think perhaps this fear came about one night many years ago, when I was coming back from a recording studio in France. My car was hit by one whose driver had fallen asleep at the wheel. It was a near-fatal accident in which three other cars were involved. My car spun around on the highway several times and ended up facing the opposite direction. I shall never forget the feeling of the car being out of control and the sound of screeching tyres and metal grating on metal and bits and pieces flying in all directions. When the car finally came to a halt, I just sat there in a daze, thinking: '*Mon Dieu*, that was a close shave!' The car was a total wreck, but neither I nor any of the other drivers were seriously injured.

'It was obviously not my time,' I thought.

I really do believe that each of us has an allotted time and this belief only makes it all the more imperative for me to achieve all the things I want to achieve. None of us knows when that time will come – it could be today, tomorrow, any time – and these days, when I'm getting on and off planes and in and out of cars every few hours, I think about all the things I still want to do in life. I don't think I will ever feel that I have done them but, at the end of the day, when I finally look death in the face, I know I will say a heartfelt '*Je ne regrette rien*,' because I have had so many happy, out-of-this-world moments in my life.

My life has always been more about work than play, but as a Frenchman I have always found time for love and romance. Where matters of the heart are concerned I soon learned that I needed to proceed with caution

One of the very best was the birth of my best friend Benjamin's baby Chloé. Benjamin is like a brother to me, my soul-mate, a truly beautiful person who life has not always treated well. I respect and admire him so much for overcoming the difficulties he has had in his life and for pulling through to be the kind of man he is today. Sadly, I was on tour with Il Divo when his wife Elena gave birth to Chloé and I couldn't be there, but Benjamin sent me pictures of the baby, taken a few minutes after she was born, and when I looked at these I just couldn't believe how beautiful, how perfect she was and how emotional I felt for Ben.

My life has always been more about work than play, but as a Frenchman I have always found time for love and romance. Where matters of the heart are concerned I soon learned that I needed to proceed with caution, not something that came naturally to my Latin temperament. In many ways I am typically French and am led by my heart rather than my head. The problem is that I find people lovable most of the time and fall in love easily. All the girls I have ever loved have been special and, in one way or another, inspirational. Catherine, for example, who was my girlfriend for two years, was the person who encouraged me to join Il Divo, so I owe her a lot. Ours was such a passionate relationship that it was inevitable that in the end we would burn ourselves out. Girls like the men in their lives to have interesting jobs, but they also want to spend time with them and Catherine found the business I was in impossible. However, she was – and still is – a very special person in my life, and I want the best for her. We've remained good friends and I still call her sometimes. After that relationship came to an end, it took me two years to find out who I was and rebuild myself.

Finding true love was even trickier after I became a member of Il Divo. The trouble then became: 'How can I be sure that this person loves me for who I am, not for what I do?' I never really lost my belief in love, though, and I am now head over heels again and ready to settle down and have a family.

I always thought my ideal woman would be someone who had confidence in herself, who had an inner strength and serenity, who was intellectual but didn't feel the need to prove this all the time, and I have found all these qualities in Renée Murphy, a lovely Melbourne girl whom I met when she was working as the publicist for Sony BMG in Australia. We have only been together for just over eighteen months, but we are so well suited, and I feel totally happy and have never felt so secure in a relationship. Finding your soul mate is a gift from above. There were some difficulties at first because I was afraid, given previous hurtful experiences, to get too deeply involved and because of the distance and the nature of this business. But one day I thought, 'Are you going to let what happened before ruin every relationship you have from now on? This is the best chance for me. I've found my other half. I've found the one.' I knew that I didn't want to lose her and that I would never find another woman quite as beautiful as Renée is in every way.

One of the best moments in my life was when I proposed to Renée on 1 June 2007. I knew that she would want to be asked in a very simple way and I had considered doing it in Venice a few weeks before, during a romantic weekend. But it didn't feel right and I knew I would have to wait for the right moment, without too much planning. After carrying the engagement ring with me for months that moment finally arrived. We were sitting outside a pub in Brussels on a warm summer night, chatting about life and what we wanted to do together. I asked her what was the craziest thing she would like to do with me. She gave me a suitably offhand reply and then asked me the same question. I told her I wanted her to marry me. She thought I was kidding, and started laughing in a nervous way, but I insisted that I was serious. I told her, 'Look, I'm going to put something into your hand that will prove it to you.' It was the box containing the ring. She thought it was cufflinks that a fan had given me and assumed that I was still joking. That made it even more magical and funny. My heart was beating so fast and I was so nervous until she opened the box and said 'yes.' I was elated.

I love surprising her. I flew her family to Paris during our first Christmas together, her first away from home, as Christmas is important to us as a family festivity. Her birthday is 13 December, so it was extra special for her to have her family with her. It took her completely by surprise and although I wasn't there to see her face, I heard her tears of joy over the telephone. I thought that was the least I could do for the woman I love who has left so much behind to come and live with me.

The best moments are when you're just walking along, holding someone's hand.

One of the most romantic things I have done for Renée was when she was spending some days with me in Miami while I was there on tour with Il Divo. It was a special date for us and I had bought her a vintage watch to mark our first year spent together. I placed it in a small box, which in turn I put in a gigantic box.

Just as it got dark outside, I asked Renée to meet me on the beach in ten minutes. All wasn't really as I had planned – it was blowing a gale-force wind and when she arrived I was standing in the only bit of light I could find, next to a smelly rubbish bin on the sand! She just laughed and said, 'Sébastien what are you up to?' I gave her the box and she started to unwrap it, her eyes as big as saucers. She was digging around in the enormous box, saying, 'But there's nothing here, Séb.' Then she found the small box, unwrapped it and just loved the watch. It's a very special moment for both of us. I will never forget the way we were looking at each other, the perfect connection. It was so romantic but remembering the wind and the rubbish bin still makes us laugh!

I love choosing and giving presents, but I never forget that the most unforgettable romantic moments are not about gifts. The best moments are when you're just walking along, holding someone's hand, or when you exchange a certain smile, a magical moment, a connection, a sparkle in your eyes like Renée and I had on the beach.

Romance is about the magic two people in love create just by being together. Love gives you wings. And thank you to Renée for making me feel like I can fly so far with you by my side. I am a very lucky man.

So these days I can hardly believe my own good fortune. Despite all the wonderful things I have experienced with Il Divo, there hasn't been a moment that has surpassed Renée saying 'yes', or holding my best friend's baby in my arms for the first time. And I guess that will remain the case until I hold my own son or daughter. I can't wait.

> The World Cup final really was a *very* special moment for me because it was between France and Italy. Even though Italy won the Cup . . .

That's not to say that there haven't been some extraordinary moments in terms of my Il Divo career. One of my favourite early memories was when we were invited to sing live when the Oxford Street Christmas lights were switched on in 2004. There, on a stage erected outside Selfridges, we joined London's Mayor, Ken Livingstone, Olympic medallist Sir Steve Redgrave, Britain's gold medal-winning relay team and the actress Emma Watson, who plays Hermione in the Harry Potter movies. It was a fabulous occasion because this event coincided with the day that London submitted its plans to host the 2012 Olympics and everybody was in a party mood. Who would have thought that a frog would be so embraced by his new adopted country, the UK?

Another memorable day was when we performed at the Henley Festival in the UK in 2005. There was nowhere better to do our first full-length live performance than on a floating stage on the Thames. There were so many of our fans there to welcome us, and when we finished singing our first number, accompanied by the Heart of England Orchestra, they gave us rapturous applause. We then encored with 'Unchained Melody', which the crowd loved. It was just wonderful – we reached giddy heights that night – and the event really set us up for going to Sweden to work on the recording of our second album, *Ancora*.

Henley was a foretaste of so many similar moments. One of these was teaming up with Toni Braxton to sing 'The Time of Our Lives', the song that was used as the official 2006 FIFA World Cup anthem and performed at the championship's opening ceremony in Munich and the final in Berlin. It was such a thrill to record with Toni, a six-time Grammy Award-winner with an amazing, husky alto voice. The way she combines jazz, gospel and blues numbers is second to none. The World Cup final really was a *very* special moment for me because it was between France and Italy. Even though Italy won the Cup, it was a thrill to perform in a stadium where so many French people would have given their last euro to be that day.

I was sitting in the V.I.P. area, watching the game with some friends who'd come from over from France. Nobody could come close to imagining how we felt when France was awarded the first penalty kick. I was so beside myself with excitement, I jumped clean out of my seat. As I did so, somebody behind me muttered in a very disgruntled voice, 'Could you, please, *sit down.*' I was too happy to take offence and just continued enjoying the moment. Then when France scored and I leapt up in the air again, the same guy said, 'Are you happy now? Can you sit down again?' This was too much for me and I made to answer him back. 'Sit down, Séb! Shut up!' my friends kept hissing, trying to indicate something. I looked over my shoulder to see who had been so unpleasant to me. It was Gerhard Schröder, Germany's ex-Chancellor!

One of the highlights of the early days of Il Divo was our success in America, which amazed me. I really didn't think Americans would embrace our kind of music, and I was so proud when I was proved wrong, particularly as I have family there.

One of the highlights of the early days of Il Divo was our success in America, which amazed me. I really didn't think Americans would embrace our kind of music, and I was so proud when I was proved wrong, particularly as I have family there. It's such a big country – something that can only be truly appreciated when touring over there. What I enjoy most about the US is that its people are so vocal, so very loud!

I loved being there when we did our twenty-date tour with Barbra Streisand. People kept saying to us, 'How will her improvisations fit in with your more structured approach?' But we really enjoyed the challenge, liked the fact that we were never quite sure what she was going to do next. She enjoys interacting with the audience and giving vent to her strong political opinions. When she included a sketch about George Bush in one of the shows, someone started heckling her. 'If you only want to listen to my music,' she replied, 'buy my albums. If you want to come and see me, it's part of the package.'

The very first moment I met her I fell under her spell. I completely understand why everyone adores her. She is everything I would love to be as a performer – grace personified – and the way she talks makes me wish English was my first language, which is quite something for a Frenchman to admit. When she plays the piano she sometimes strikes a few wrong notes or chords, but the effect is still awesome. As far as I'm concerned, she's magical.

Another mind-blowing Il Divo moment – and, in truth, I could go on listing them forever – was when we were presented with impressive glass plaques by SYCO/Sony BMG for over 10 million albums sold. The way we have been embraced just really hit home to me, and this was even before the release of *Siempre*.

> Looking back at the schedule for our 2007 World Tour, I can hardly believe that we went to so many countries and played at so many different venues.

Looking back at the schedule for our 2007 World Tour, I can hardly believe that we went to so many countries and played at so many different venues. To give people an idea of how hard we guys work, I cannot resist listing them here. In the first five months of the tour, we performed in Kuala Lumpur, Singapore, Manila, Hong Kong, Shanghai, Seoul, Tokyo, Osaka, Sydney, Brisbane, Adelaide, Melbourne, Sun City, Cape Town, Johannesburg, Halifax, Toronto, Montreal, Ottawa, Winnipeg, Calgary, Edmonton, Kelowna, Vancouver, Victoria, Cardiff, London, Newcastle, Glasgow, Birmingham, Manchester, Sheffield, Rotterdam, Antwerp, Oberhausen, Helsinki, Stockholm, Copenhagen, Hamburg, Zurich, Vienna, Ljubljana, Lisbon, Paris, Belfast and Dublin. How did we cope with all that globe-trotting and still remain smiling and on top form? That was easy. We love our work, love our fans and there's nothing we enjoy more than singing live on stage.

World tours, amazing venues, sell-out concerts; none of us could have dreamed that Il Divo would be such a phenomenal success. I honestly don't think any of us had such high hopes, and I know for sure that when everything started up in the UK I never expected our first album to be a number one. Then when that success continued around the world, I thought, 'I can't believe it!' And do you know what? I'm still thinking that.

Urs
I Believe In You

There have been many remarkable moments in my life, but none to top the one that stands out in my memory. It occurred a few years ago, just after I had finished a performance of *Simone Boccanegra* in Salzburg, Austria. The minute I left the stage, I leapt astride my old Harley Davidson and rode 1,200 kilometres throughout the night, for eleven hours. Why? Because I was in love and wanted to be with my then girlfriend in Amsterdam.

I knew that night what it was like to be king of the road and experience total elation and freedom. All my senses heightened, I felt in tune with the wind and rain, the sun rising, the dawn of a new day. It was a never-to-be-forgotten experience, one of those rare occasions when you truly know what it is to be alive.

I am not sure if the following is fact or fiction, but somebody once told me that the Ancient Greeks only ever asked one question when a man or woman died: 'Did they have passion?' I can only say that, thanks to that memorable motorbike ride, I understand *why* that question is considered so important, and I can answer, 'Yes, I do have passion in my life.'

There were five kids in my family – three girls, my brother and me – and when my dad walked out on us, my mum, who was a milliner, had to pull us through single-handedly, and she did. She succeeded in giving us all a happy childhood in the village of Willisau, Switzerland.

My abiding memory of my father stems from when I was about seven years old. One wintry day he took me to see the ducks and herons that had flocked to a lake close to our village. The lake was frozen over and as I broke loose from him and ran on to one section of the ice, it suddenly shattered and I plunged down into the lake's depths. As it closed over my head, my eyes, ears, nose and mouth filled up with freezing cold water. Before I had time to fully realise what was happening, my dad reached down into the water and yanked me out. Just for a moment, though, it had been touch and go, and if he hadn't been so quick to act, I might not be here to tell this tale. In a country with cold winters like Switzerland, everyone is aware of ice being a hazard. I distinctly remember that we had a book in which there were illustrations showing what to do when somebody falls through it. It frightened us a bit as little children but it certainly did not keep us from 'walking on the ice' whenever we had a chance.

Once we were over the initial shock of our father leaving us, we managed to survive without him in our lives. I was always very aware, though, of how hard my mother had to work and how little money we had, and I always tried to help. My first vacation job was in a supermarket when I was eight years old, and I have never stopped working since. I did a spell in a furniture firm when I was eleven, started distributing newspapers when I was fourteen, worked all through my school holidays, then got a job as a fork-lift truck driver in a warehouse for eleven months.

I have always tried to help. My first vacation job was in a supermarket when I was eight years old, and I have never stopped working since.

Fender
STRATOCASTER
RoHS

Throughout my student days, although I was always very fortunate to get good sponsorship grants, I continued to take on all sorts of part-time jobs, doing every imaginable type of work in the building trade – I thoroughly enjoyed that kind of physical labour. Even before I started my professional voice studies I sang a lot of oratorio concerts and recitals, which allowed me to live on whatever money I earned, and I still had a great life. Ever since those days, I've never been afraid of not being able to make a living. From as far back as I can remember, my mother has always expressed her belief in me, so, thanks to her, I grew up believing in myself, believing I could do anything. I'm very proud of that, and it's one reason why I enjoy singing the song 'I Believe In You'. It reminds me of my mother, of those days.

Perhaps because my father left when I was so young, I was always determined that when I grew up I would be a big, strong man, just like the knights and Vikings I saw in paintings and movies and read about in books, someone who could cope in any situation. To this day, people who are in control of their destinies, on top of situations, fascinate me.

I have always counted myself very lucky to have grown up in Switzerland.

I have always counted myself very lucky to have grown up in Switzerland. Situated at the centre of western Europe, but outside of it politically, it is a very special, beautiful country, and I am so proud of it. Switzerland's glaciers are sometimes referred to as 'Europe's water towers' because they supply some of western Europe's largest rivers, and the mountain ranges – the Jura in the west and the Swiss Alps in the south and east – are magnificent.

Willisau, our village, only had a population of about six and a half thousand, but when I was growing up, there were five motorcycle gangs there. I guess this was just because a lot of the people live up in the hills and a motorcycle is a cheap and handy mode of transport. But it was a symbol of freedom and independence as well, and it's not really surprising then that motorbikes and motorbike culture became, and have remained, passions of mine.

I was so keen on motorbikes, I bought my first one at seventeen, even though in Switzerland you have to be eighteen to ride one on the road. I only took it out at night to practice without anyone knowing, not even my parents. Three years later I bought my first Harley Davidson from money saved up for years from all my jobs. It was a fantastic long fork chopper with high handlebars. I was so sad when I moved to Holland and I had to sell it, but I needed the money to continue my studies abroad. Being a student meant that money was always tight. Even when I was thirty, all I could afford was an old seventies Honda Goldwing for five hundred pounds, which I restored myself. That motorbike is superb. I still own it and I am very proud of it.

This particular love of my life first got off the ground when I was sixteen and went abroad for the first time in my life. Me and three other guys from school went on a summer holiday to the south of France with our bicycles and somehow ended up in quite a rough biker camping ground. The big Harleys were roaring all through the night and one morning when we left the place to go down to the beach for a swim, two bikes came toward us against the rising sun. I can still see their silhouettes clearly... and I was hooked forever!

My chief passions have always been my music and my motorbikes. To this day, I am fascinated by custom choppers, and no matter where I am or what I am doing, if I see or hear one in the street, I have to stop and take a look.

My chief passions have always been my music and my motorbikes. To this day, I am fascinated by custom choppers, and no matter where I am or what I am doing, if I see or hear one in the street, I have to stop and take a look.

I started customizing my own bikes when I was a teenager, and I found it inspirational. Twenty years on, I still have a lot of ideas in my head about how I would like to modify this or that bike. It's just something that keeps my brain occupied. Then, of course, there is the sheer joy of riding them. I love the sound of a Harley, which is completely different to that of a Japanese-made racing bike. A well-tuned Harley has a satisfyingly deep, earthy roar. Sometimes when I ride one of my big bikes along a country road, I lean my body over as far as I can to one side and watch its front wheel spinning over the asphalt. I just love that feeling of weight and power, of having 300 kilos of heavy metal vibrating beneath me, while controlling it with just a flick of the wrist.

Inevitably, being young and feeling wild and free on a motorbike, always wanting to push my road-handling skills to the limit, I had several near-death experiences. Those are common enough in ordinary road-surface conditions, but even more so on icy roads like the ones in Switzerland. When you plough into snow drifts or hit patches of black ice, your heart really races a marathon and the adrenalin courses in an unstoppable stream through your veins. After a few years, however, when I started taking my girlfriend, one of my sisters or even my mother on the back for a nice ride in the sun, I realized the responsibility I had for my passengers which made me change my riding style. I think I am a very cautious and secure rider nowadays.

Having said all that, the scariest moment I've ever experienced was not on the road, but during a bungee jump off a cable car in the Swiss Alps. I like to think of myself as quite a brave man who's up for anything, but once I'd leapt out of the cabin, I screamed my head off. At that instant, you don't feel the bungee rope around your ankles and think, 'It's okay, I'm safe,' you are just aware that you are just out in the open air with nothing to hold on to, falling to earth. Despite my fear, that jump was a brilliant birthday present from my dad and I would do it over again anytime.

Surprisingly, given the dangers I have exposed myself to, I have never broken any bones, but, as I am a romantic by nature, I have often had my heart broken.

Surprisingly, given the dangers I have exposed myself to, I have never broken any bones, but, as I am a romantic by nature, I have often had my heart broken. I fell head-over-heels in love many times when I was a teenager, and I was absolutely devastated when the girl rejected me. When I was about twenty-four, I remember being very attracted to a girl at the Amsterdam Conservatory. But she just wouldn't take me seriously. She'd play with my feelings, pick me up and throw me away again according to her mood. She treated love as if it were a game, and that really broke my heart. It took me at least two years to get over that.

Those two early experiences didn't have any long-term damaging effects, but they probably did contribute to the difficulties I had making the first move when I was in my mid to late twenties. To some people, such things come naturally; it's just a matter of going out and meeting somebody and the rest is easy. But I was very inhibited and I found it hard to start up conversations with girls I was attracted to. Still I haven't been single since I was nineteen, so it must have happened somehow. Nowadays of course things are completely different. I guess, if I was single, standing on stage and being a singer is quite some first move.

Money, once I have enough to cover my basic needs, has never been that important to me, and certainly never a prime motivation in my life. Despite not having a father during my formative years, I've always felt secure. Perhaps that's because I come from a large family and I always knew that if things got really hard, I would still have somewhere to lay my head. I still feel like that today. Even now that I've achieved the kind of success I could never have achieved, I still know that come what may, there will always be someone there for me.

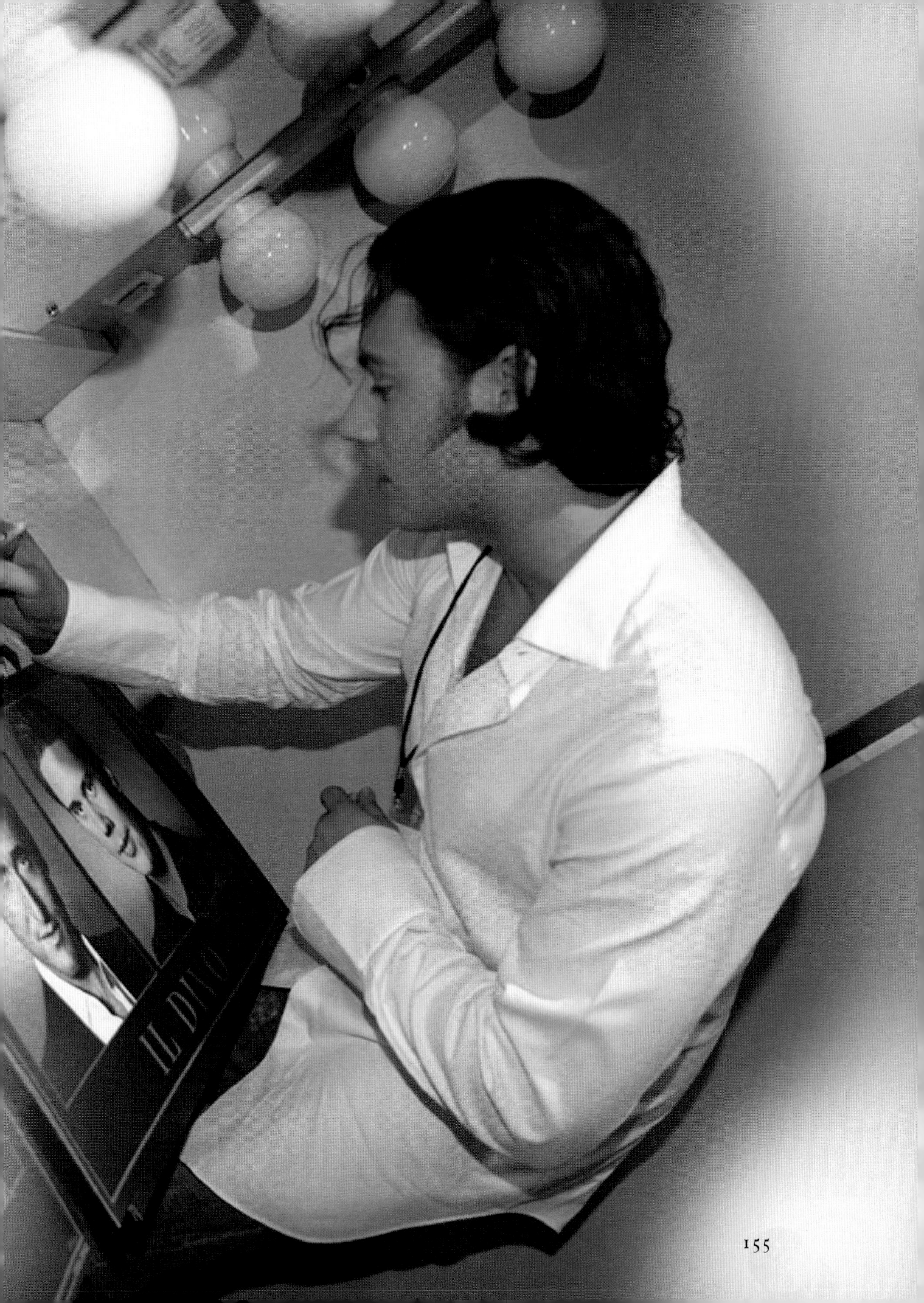
IL DIVO

It certainly wasn't the money – or the pursuit of fame – that made me decide to audition for Il Divo. What actually appealed to me about it was the challenge: a challenge which might, I decided, persuade me to abandon an already successful career in opera and instead grasp an opportunity to take my voice to a larger audience.

It certainly wasn't the money – or the pursuit of fame – that made me decide to audition for Il Divo. What actually appealed to me about it was the challenge

By the time that possibility came along, I had been living in Amsterdam for more than eight years. I originally moved there to further my classical voice training after getting my Masters degree in Switzerland. Before graduating from the Amsterdam Conservatory I started working at the Dutch opera. There I got the chance to closely observe some of the world's greatest singers and conductors rehearsing and performing. It was a priceless experience for an ambitious young singer. At the conservatory, I also benefited from private tuition with the late Swedish tenor Gösta Winbergh and the French tenor Christian Papis.

The Il Divo audition came about in December 2003, at a time when I was singing with a vocal ensemble that had been specially cast for a stage production of Handel's oratorium *Samson* at the Amsterdam Muziektheater. An English countertenor in that production told me about a record company in London that was looking for lyric tenors. 'They are searching for people with southern European looks,' he said, 'and voices that aren't too heavy.' He didn't know precisely what the project was, but thought it might be something to do with a crossover group.

'You could be just right for it,' he added. 'Why not send off your CV and a couple of photographs?'

As I was a freelance singer always on the lookout for the next interesting job, I decided to do just that, and very soon after was invited by SYCO, a UK record label, to an audition. I was told they would fly me to London, pick me up at the airport and take me to the office in Fulham where I would be presented to Simon Cowell. I had never heard that name before and had no idea who Simon was. But funnily enough I had recently started thinking about leaving Amsterdam and moving on to another big European city so I thought this would be an interesting chance to see a bit of London.

The audition, which was held in Simon's office, was very peculiar. There was no piano, no accompanist of any kind, just a large desk and two sofas on either side of the room with six or seven people sitting on them, some from SYCO and some from a management team that was involved in the audition process.

Once we'd all sat down, Simon talked to me for about forty-five minutes. He explained that what he had in mind was a group of classically trained singers who would sing pop songs, and he played me a couple of demo tapes. One song, 'Feelings', had been written for Celine Dion, who had decided, for one reason or another, not to release it. Simon said he would like to record it with his new group.

While he was speaking, I was growing more and more sceptical and I asked him, sounding rather incredulous, 'You want me to sing this kind of music with my lyric voice?' I emphasised that I was a classically trained singer, and that I wasn't prepared to do anything else.

'That's *exactly* why you are here,' he said.

As I was happy with my life and my operatic career, which was growing slowly but steadily, I was not at all sure about what Simon was asking me to do. 'Well, I'm happy to try it,' I hesitated, 'but I can't imagine it's going to work.'

So finally I stood up and sang for him. The aria I chose was Donizetti's 'Una Furtiva Lagrima', from *L'Elisir d'Amore*, and I sang it without any accompaniment. Simon sat behind his desk smoking a cigarette – off-putting when you've only experienced the respect of a classical jury.

The aria I chose was Donizetti's 'Una Furtiva Lagrima', from *L'Elisir d'Amore*, and I sang it without any accompaniment. Simon sat behind his desk smoking a cigarette

'Brilliant,' he said, as the last note faded. 'I *love* it.'

He then came out from behind his desk, shook my hand, wished me a good flight home and said he would call me the next day.

The call from SYCO that was to change my life came the next evening. They told me that they'd love me to join the group (the name Il Divo hadn't been discussed yet) and that recordings were scheduled to begin in January. A contract and an advance would follow once the financial details were finalised.

Even having passed the audition and been offered the job, I remained sceptical. It took three weeks before I finally reached a decision and phoned SYCO back with a positive answer. I was only too aware that I was taking a big gamble with my operatic career. My name was just becoming known in classical circles and *nobody* could have known at that stage how well Il Divo would do.

There were a few reasons that helped me decide to join the group. I sought the advice of a lot of renowned opera singers I had worked with in Amsterdam and everyone thought it sounded like a fantastic opportunity. They all agreed the opera business had become very difficult in the last few years and even established artists were having to fight much harder to make a decent living out of singing. I also decided that it could be the perfect time for me to throw myself into an experiment like this. I had been the lead singer of a hard rock band when I was a teenager – a fact that surprised a lot of people when we stepped into the public eye for the first time as a classical-crossover quartet – so being on a pop stage was not new to me. Also, as far as the opera world was concerned, at thirty-two I was still relatively young and could comfortably take a few years out without being too old to return, provided I kept my lyric voice in a good and healthy shape.

Having started out at the age of fifteen as a rock singer with no particular vocal training, then studying classical music as a teacher and singer for almost ten years, bringing all that knowledge and experience together in a crossover act began to feel like making a full circle.

Just two days after Carlos, David, Sébastien and I were brought together, we started recording the first album, *Il Divo*. Nobody knew how the tracks would turn out. At that time, we had only met each other once before, and we didn't know anything about each other or each other's voices. For three classically trained singers and one pop singer the creation of a new sound was very much a step-by-step process. All we and the producers had were a few demo tapes of pop tunes and Simon Cowell's expectation that we would make them sound amazing. How? 'You're the singers. Make it work!'

This stage of Il Divo's career was very relaxed for the four of us. We hadn't yet released an album, we were unknown and anything could happen. But from the record company's point of view there was a lot riding on Il Divo. Nevertheless, they gave us as long as we needed to get it right. Thanks to the release dates of our first album being staggered, we had ample time to fly to the different countries and spend a few days in each doing promotional work, interviews and performances. We had no idea then that those days would not last, that our future albums would be released all around the world at more or less the same time, and that everything would become much more pressurized. On the following albums, we would find ourselves visiting up to three different countries in a day or flying three times back and forth over the Atlantic within a week, in order to put in as much promotional work and as many personal appearances as we could. Perhaps it is just as well that we did not know this in the early days!

Carlos, David, Sébastien and I obviously didn't choose each other as partners, and maybe we wouldn't have, had we been involved in the decision. Having become Simon's protégés, we were thrown in at the deep end, or perhaps I should say stirred into the melting pot. Four guys who all knew their own minds could have been a recipe for disaster, but, although it has been touch and go sometimes, we have gotten to know each other and learned how to make the necessary allowances and adjustments.

I am quite typically Swiss in some ways. I'm very private and a bit distant, quite complex as a personality, and I like things to be neat and done in a proper manner.

Carlos is a very forceful guy, he is loud and proud, and he is not always easy to be around. But his voice is absolutely fabulous. I once heard a recording of him singing when he was eight years old and it was just there, even at that early age. He's a real talent. The same counts for Sébastien. He has a wonderful, natural voice with a beautiful tone and smoothness to it. Personally – and forgive me for the cliché – he is *very* French. Like so many French people, he has a tendency to be dramatic, to make mountains out of molehills. David is a good guy, smart, very open and concerned with everyone's well-being, never really aggressive or offensive. He can also be a big baby at times, which can be either hilariously funny or slightly annoying, I guess depending on my own mood. But he's the one I can really talk to.

The truth is, we have our difficulties, but I like them all really.

As for me, I guess I am quite typically Swiss in some ways. I'm very private and a bit distant, quite complex as a personality, and I like things to be neat and done in a proper manner. That has much to do with my upbringing and education. It's part of the Swiss mentality to be very correct and precise, at least on the outside. Inside, I guess, we're all human. People have often told me that gaining access to the real me is difficult – impossible sometimes. One of my good points, however, is that I am very patient. These days, I mostly just try to be myself and remain very cool, calm, collected and sensible, and I hope I bring these qualities to our group discussions.

I think that if Carlos, David, Sébastien and I were all the same nationality, we would understand each other more easily. As it is, the fact that we come from such different cultures can sometimes create problems. We all have somewhat extreme personalities, and there are times when we have to tread quite carefully with each other if we are to avoid misinterpretations and hurt feelings. Not everyone always does, and I'm sure the other guys have no idea of how carefully I sometimes tread.

Generally we are relaxed, make fun of ourselves and each other and have a good time together. When it comes to taking important decisions as a group, that's where the disagreements start. Things can get pretty heated up with all that ego in one room, especially given the stress of travelling, rehearsing and dealing with all the highs and lows of this amazing rollercoaster ride. But all this passion and energy is also what we bring on stage together, and to me it is clearly one part of the magic of Il Divo. And if everything was harmonious and beautiful, all sweetness and light, day in day out, that would be *really* boring. I've learned how to deal with my frustration and anger and, in truth, I wouldn't hurt a hair on their heads.

I've also come to accept that I'm a person who likes – and needs – a lot of space around me. There are often moments when I recognize that I have had enough of other people for the time being. It's not just the other guys, it's everybody. I'm really not good at being around a bunch of people all the time. I very rarely go out with the group outside of our work schedule. I certainly join everybody for dinner if it is somebody's birthday, for example, but in general I prefer to go to the gym for a workout, walk around the city or practice guitar. Anything that just gets my mind off Il Divo.

Playing the guitar is one of my passions in life, and there is so much more I want to achieve with it. I've discovered some time ago that the power of heavy metal, which I like so much, was there in classical music centuries ago. When I listen to big operas or symphonies, I can hear that the rhythms, the accents, the fast tremolos, even the chord progressions are all there. There's nothing new about hard rock.

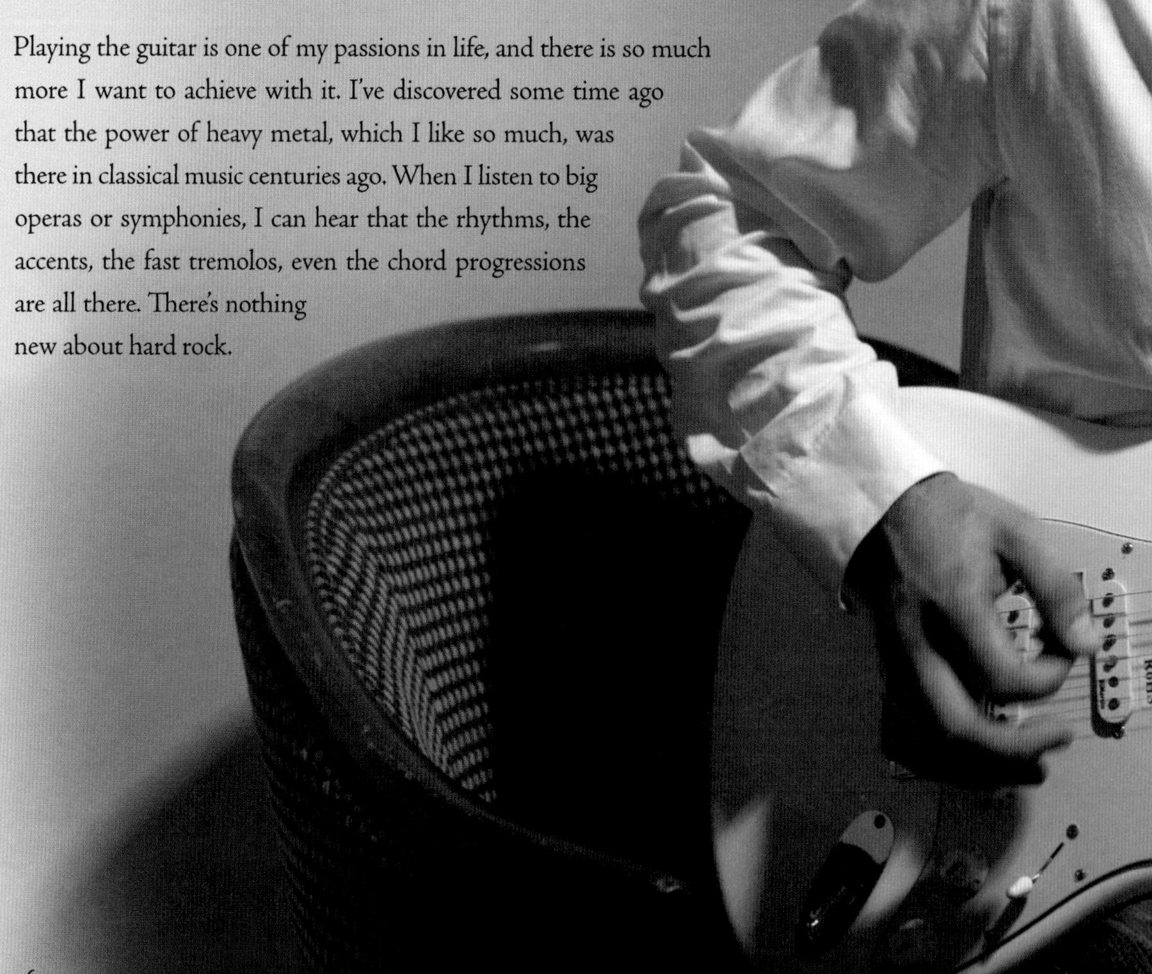

I now know most of the good guitar shops around the world, although I haven't seen much of the cities they are situated in.

URS
SEB
Carlos
DAVID

But my passion for the guitar knows no bounds. My collection is steadily growing and I guess it says something about me that I now know most of the good guitar shops around the world, although I haven't seen much of the cities they are situated in.

From the first moment our Il Divo odyssey has been a huge adventure. When we started we all had the same ambition: to grow as artists and singers and make the crossover to other audiences. And we have succeeded in both. Since the first memorable Il Divo performance at the Henley Festival in the summer of 2005, we have performed numerous shows around the world. I think – and I'm almost certain that Carlos, David and Sébastien would agree – that the moments when we stand on a stage together and perform live are the ones that bring out the very best in us.

When we started we all had the same ambition: to grow as artists and singers and make the crossover to other audiences. And we have succeeded in both.

I just love singing on a stage. The emotion of the songs sends shivers down my spine. I *feel* music, am passionate about it. In that instant it's all I need. There are some songs, like 'Caruso', when I just stand there and think, 'Oh, God, this is *so* wonderful.' I wouldn't care if the hall was empty. I used to say this to Carlos, Sébastien and David in the early days of Il Divo, but I don't think they really believed me. Still it's true that I don't need the whole fame thing; it is the process of making music that satisfies a deep need in me. I get so much from it. I am never able to sleep until two or three o'clock in the morning after a performance, because it's such an adrenalin rush. When I lived in Amsterdam, singing operas, I would go home afterwards and listen to the whole piece again until the early hours of the morning. My friends and colleagues used to think I was completely crazy. But that's what music does to me.

Fortunately we're lucky enough not to have to worry about empty concert halls. Our first world tour saw us playing to more than a hundred thousand people in the British Isles alone, and the second one was even bigger. We would never have got the chance to perform to that many people if we had played safe and rested on our laurels in the opera world.

Since those early days, we have gained a lot of experience and knowledge about the pop business. If what we do continues to work for our fans, it will be because we always put our bodies, hearts and souls into it. Not everybody realizes that Il Divo originated in the UK, even though none of us is British. But every time we go back, we get such a warm welcome from our loyal fans. It really feels like Il Divo's natural home.

In the very beginning, especially before we released our first record, the few trips we made to television studios were an absolute nightmare. We would be called in early in the morning for a sound check even though our three-minute performance would not actually go out until six in the evening. Then we would have to spend the whole day just sitting around with ten people in a pokey dressing room with absolutely nothing to do. We would have left our hotel in the dark and not have come out of the television studio until after the sun had already gone down, missing all the daylight for the sake of a couple of minutes on the screen. Nowadays, most of our visits to TV studios are much quicker. We simply can't do that anymore, just waiting and doing nothing.

> Not everybody realizes that Il Divo originated in the UK, even though none of us is British.

We have made repeat appearances on a lot of TV shows in the past few years. In particular, the GMTV studio in London has almost become our second home when we are in the UK. We know the space, the equipment and the faces of the people who work there so well that going there almost feels like going for a walk before breakfast.

Doing sound checks in television studios can be very difficult, because the equipment isn't usually as sophisticated as that which we carry on tour with us. Also TV studios are often geared towards one singer, rather than four voices given equal precedence, so we do whatever we can to make things easier for ourselves. Sébastien and I both use in-ear monitors whenever the studios can provide the technical facilities to do so. It makes mixing of the stage sound much easier, as the engineer only has to balance David and Carlos's voices. Séb and I both have our own mixes in our ears, which are tailored to our personal requests without bothering anybody else.

When we're in the recording studio for the production of the albums, we never actually record together. Only one of us enters the booth at any one time. That's not very romantic unfortunately, but a technical necessity to reach the highest possible quality and purity of the sound.

Recordings have become very much easier, compared to the first time, because, with all the experience from touring we have gotten to know each others' voices so well now. Sharing the leads and arranging the harmonies has become much more obvious, and our producers have a clearer idea of Il Divo's sound than they had in the beginning.

I used to find it so depressing having to sit around the studio all day, waiting until I was needed. Sometimes I turned up at ten o'clock in the morning and didn't actually record anything until ten in the evening. So I have started staying in hotels that are in easy walking distance from the studio. On the first day of a recording session, we all go to the studio together to listen to a few tracks and then decide who is going to start. Carlos normally prefers to go in first. So if he is followed by Sébastien and David, I know I won't be needed for the next two days and can go and work out or go sightseeing. If the schedule changes I'm still just a phone call away.

Recordings have become very much easier because we have gotten to know each others' voices so well now

When we recorded 'I Believe In You', which was written by Per Magnusson and David Kreuger, with Celine Dion for *Ancora*, Celine recorded her part of the track in Montreal. It would have been nice for us to meet up but it wasn't really necessary. We did have the pleasure of singing with her a couple of months later in Paris. We were there promoting our respective albums, and Celine was often on the same TV shows as us. There were some very amusing moments with her security guard, who was always standing on duty outside her dressing-room door. A really big, muscular guy, he had an unmistakable 'don't mess with me or my lady' look on his face whenever we walked by. It was only after he came to understand who we were – and know that Celine was perfectly safe with us – that he started smiling at us, which was soon followed by hearty handshakes.

As for Celine herself, we didn't really have a chance to have a proper chat and get to know her, but during the first show we did together, she came over and greeted us with a kiss on the cheek. We started chatting away and making silly jokes together. She was such a lovely, warm person that I felt we'd known each other forever, and as she's such a fantastic singer, I think I was almost a bit star-struck!

But despite the fame, the fans, the touring, the television performances, meeting big artists like Celine Dion, and everything else that has happened to me since I joined Il Divo, I have always remained more concerned with the music than with being a star.

When I'm performing on stage, all my energy and focus go into making each note I'm singing as beautiful and as expressive as I can, always with a cautious eye on my technique, so I don't hurt myself. My parts in Il Divo cover a very big range, and switching around between the lowest and the highest voice in a quartet is quite a challenge. There's a lot of heavy singing in the finales of the songs, and I think if we didn't all know exactly what we're doing, we could very easily damage our voices, particularly with the number of performances on a six-month tour.

Right from the start, Carlos, David, Sébastien and I always wanted to be appreciated more for our music and not for how we look

I like being part of group. I have always shared the stage with other artists. Even when I did *lied* recitals, I was with a pianist. Throughout my career, I can't remember a single moment when I felt it was just me. It's always been an 'us' situation, so sharing the stage with the three other guys has, in a sense, come naturally to me. It is very comforting and reassuring to know that you're not alone up there and there's always somebody to lean on when you're feeling a bit rough.

Right from the start, Carlos, David, Sébastien and I always wanted to be appreciated for our music and not for how we look, and, of course, we have been depressed at times by some of the critics claiming that we are a conveyor-belt, manufactured group that make it harder for other acts to break into the music industry. But every time one of these critics says something along these lines, our fans respond in droves by helping us to break more and more records. Never have so many people been so ready to reassure us that they *know* that we are not just another cog in the Simon Cowell music machine, that we each proved that we have talent long before we joined Il Divo, and that our already established careers in the music business speak for themselves. Of course, because we are classically trained, we find it frustrating at times when we're not taken seriously by some journalists, but, in the end, it's always difficult for us to take the criticisms too much to heart when we have such wonderful fans.

We have come such a long way in such a short time that I think we have now reached a point where we can more or less deal with anything that is thrown at us. TV studios, cameras and journalists don't frighten us anymore. And even when we have arguments about this or that, we always know that in the end, we all pull on the same string together.

Most of the journalists we meet are pleasant, but it can be irritating when you read the article later and see that they deliberately twisted something completely innocent that you told them in good faith. I was very offended by one reporter who interviewed me a couple of days after I'd had laser surgery on my eyes. When I came into the restaurant, I introduced myself and said, 'I hope you will excuse the dark glasses, but I have just had my eyes lasered.' He wasn't listening to me, though, and when he looked up, he sneered and said, 'So, what is it, then? Has your mother died?' When the article came out, I saw he'd written something along the lines of: 'Urs comes in wearing sunglasses and keeps them on in the dark restaurant during the entire interview.' And that's all he wrote about me. 'Okay,' I said to myself, 'I'll never give him another interview.' The tone he had adopted in that feature was intended to paint a very negative picture of me as an arrogant poseur, and all because I was suffering after an operation on my eyes.

I often think these days, when I am whizzing about the globe, that if I had a week to live what would I do? And there is nothing I can think of that I absolutely have to do before I die. I know that sounds terrible, but it's true. I feel as if I have accomplished so much in my life already, even beyond my wildest dreams, that I'm actually just very happy and proud. So, I wouldn't do anything special at all. Of course, there is still so much to do in my life. I would love to perfect my singing and my guitar playing and become more proficient on the piano, drums, bass and violin, all of which I also played a bit as a student, but I couldn't achieve all that in a week, could I? So, why bother?

> There is nothing I can think of that I absolutely have to do before I die. I know that sounds terrible, but it's true.

The truth is I've already seen, done and had more than I ever wished for, and although I'm sure there is much more to come which, if I knew about it, I would probably regret missing, that doesn't really worry me. I believe in seizing the day, living in the moment, I am aware of the precariousness of life. Sometimes I also think I am someone who's not very attached to life. Why is that? I certainly love being alive and I absolutely understand why many people are shocked when I talk in this way. 'Do you suffer from depression?' they ask. Not really, certainly not in a medical sense. Depressed I might have been at times, but I haven't had a suicidal thought since I was a teenager coping with unrequited love and, a bit later on, when I thought I would rather die than face not getting anywhere with my singing, never reach any of my goals. Today I see myself as one of the luckiest people on the earth.

I used to be very introverted and given to thinking about metaphysical things a lot of the time. Being a member of one of the most successful pop acts of the last few years has certainly made me a bit more sociable. But, sadly, I have far less time to just relax and enjoy life's simple pleasures since I joined Il Divo. Our existence is, out of necessity, very regimented. It's a bit like being back at school and governed by bells and clocks. We have to be very disciplined, of course, and because that is already part of my nature anyway, it is not always good for me. I'm very hard on myself, which can create difficulties because I'm inclined to expect other people to be equally hard on themselves. I am learning, though, that if people don't always live up to my standards, it's important not to be too critical. There are moments when I have to tell myself that I live my life my way, and other people live theirs in their own way, and I do not have the right to judge what is good for them and what is not. The fact remains, though, that with millions of people out there listening to our music and hundreds of thousands attending our live shows every year, we do have a tremendous responsibility, which is not always easy to live up to.

I can't emphasize enough that despite the downsides of life in Il Divo I consider myself to be a very lucky man. I have always seemed to live a dream of an existence, and if I am wise enough, I always will. I will never have to worry about having sufficient money to live on. I can – and often do – live in luxury, but I'm not dependent on it, don't need it. For me, life is not about *having*, it's about *being*, and my aim is to be as smart as I can, get myself everything I need and some of the things I want, and then just rest and be content with my lot. Whatever portion of my life I still have to come, that's how I want it to be.

I consider myself to be a very lucky man. I have always seemed to live a dream of an existence, and if I am wise enough, I always will. I will never have to worry about having sufficient money to live on.

Our second album, *Ancora*, released in November 2005, repeated what is now regarded as the historic performance of our first by again debuting at number one in the UK charts and then achieving number-one positions in a further ten countries. In the US, *Ancora*'s incredible number-one debut followed the release of our US holiday album, *The Christmas Collection*, only four months earlier, which became the highest-selling Christmas album over there for 2005.

Almost unbelievably, by the end of 2005 we had sales of ten million and eighty gold and platinum awards, and all of this was achieved without live concert appearances or traditional radio play, which we are told is almost unheard of.

The release of *Ancora* confirmed us as the most successful act launched in recent times as we had achieved sales unrivalled by any other new artist in the past few years.

Siempre, our third album, was recorded after we had completed a huge amount of touring in the first half of 2006 and had been able to get to know each other's voices really well and discover how best to blend them. As a result, we were able to record *Siempre* comparatively quickly. The whole album has a very Latin flavour to it, with all the songs, except the bonus track 'Somewhere', in Spanish or Italian.

Siempre, our third album, was recorded after we had completed a huge amount of touring in the first half of 2006 and had been able to get to know each other's voices really well and discover how best to blend them.

We managed to bring a bit more rhythm into *Siempre*, especially on the Bryan Adams cover 'Have You Ever Really Loved a Woman?' and one of the original songs, 'La Vida Sin Amor', which is our collective favourite. We are very proud of that album because we finally found a way to take Il Divo a step further on from the format that we established on our first record.

We included the song 'Without You' on *Siempre*, and as this is a track which has been covered by the likes of Harry Nilsson and Mariah Carey, we were often asked how we approached recording such a famous number. But that song was really very easy for us. The vocal arrangement of this particular one was almost a given. With its two verses followed directly by the chorus, it lent itself perfectly to sharing it between the four of us, and the way we did it, starting with the solo voices and building up to a four-part harmony and finale, suited us down to the ground.

We sang 'Somewhere' on our live tour in the first half of 2006, and we were determined to include it on *Siempre* because it is a perfect song for Il Divo. On the tour we closed the show with it and people made it very clear that they loved it. So, although it didn't really fit in with the rest of the Latin-type songs – in fact, the record company called us and questioned us about this track – we were absolutely certain that it should be included on the album as a bonus track.

I really like performing the new songs from *Siempre* on the 2007 tour. 'Without You', for example, is a joy to sing. 'Nights in White Satin', our new opener, feels just right and the ending of it is epic. The same counts for 'Musica'. I am particularly proud of this one, because John Miles, the original composer and interpreter, personally rearranged it for us. I think it is always a big compliment if another artist trusts you with one of their songs, especially, as is the case with this one, when it's their signature tune.

I am sure one of the reasons for our international success is that there is something in Il Divo for everyone. Our music is not restricted to a certain age group, nationality or culture, and because we are all from different countries and speak about eight languages between us we are able to communicate with people from all over the world when we are promoting our music. This, combined with the passion we bring to what we do, explains why we have such a broad appeal.

Speaking of passion, there is someone very special in my life who I am happy to say that I am very much in love with. She's a wonderful woman and I would love to have her at my side for the rest of my life. She is the one who pulls me through and keeps me going when I get sick and tired of it all. Somehow we just work together without any extra effort. I have often heard people say that one has to work hard at a good relationship. I guess I believed those people when I was younger. But in the back of my mind I always thought, 'No, you shouldn't have to work hard, it should just work.' And I was right.

The woman in my life has to be smart because I want to be able to talk to my partner in an intelligent way about the things that are important to me. I like women who are disciplined and able to handle themselves, and I really dislike being nagged, I guess I just had enough of it in the past. Looks, of course, are also important. Although, having said that, I really do believe that beauty is in the eye of the beholder. Whenever I've been in love, I've always thought my girlfriend was the most beautiful woman in the world. I feel the same about my mother. As far as I'm concerned, she is beautiful, and, come to that, so are my sisters. People I feel a deep love for are always beautiful in my eyes.

There is someone very special in my life who I am happy to say that I am very much in love with. She's a wonderful woman and I would love to have her at my side for the rest of my life.

I've never actually been in a situation where a partner has been untrue to me, have never experienced infidelity, but I sometimes wonder how I would deal with it. When I was young, I was very jealous and possessive, but I don't think I am any more, perhaps because none of my girlfriends has given me a reason for concern and I have therefore grown more trusting.

I was never bothered about the fact that somebody might fall in love with my image – a successful singer who has the ability to stir up emotions with his voice – rather than the real me. I accepted that this might happen some time back. But if you spend time with a person and exchange your thoughts or feelings, you just know if it's only on the surface or goes deeper.

Getting up on stage together, starting our tour all over the world in January 2007 brought us all back to what we are and what we want to be: performers. Recordings are challenging, videos and promotion are necessary, but singing live in front of a big audience is certainly what makes our hearts beat faster. The adrenalin that comes from it is quite astonishing, to me it's like a heavy workout: it's completely exhausting but enormously satisfying before, during and after you've done it.

Some people say that the applause at the end of a performance can be even better than sex, but that's not how I experience it. For me, the response of the audience has nothing to do with sex, and I don't get a sexual kick out of it. I would rather compare such moments to being like a little child again and having your mother stroke your head and say, 'Well done, sweetheart. I've always believed in you, always knew you could do anything you wanted.' To experience people showing their approval by whistling, clapping and calling out 'bravo', or racing down to the front of the stage is *very* satisfying. After all, when we are standing up there we are hoping that we are giving all the people present a really good time and that they are appreciating that. I never think of myself as a star, though. I always remain acutely aware that I am just a person, like everyone else.

Whatever the audience does, including writing us letters and giving us presents, does not surprise me. It's cool. I enjoy it. And when I look into the auditorium and see attractive women looking at me in a way that says, 'I *want* you,' I enjoy that too. What guy doesn't love to turn women on and be desired? It honestly doesn't go to my head, though. I realize that the same women will go to see another artist and probably react in the same way. That's what the fan–idol relationship is about.

The other guys and I now live on the road forty-eight weeks of the year. For the little bit of free time we get, London, which I love, serves us as a base. Once I get more time for myself, though, I don't think I'll stay in the UK. I was born and raised in Switzerland, and I still feel that that's where my roots are. I love the country and I always will. It's very possible that some day in the future I will return there and settle somewhere in the mountains for a quiet life.

The money we have made from our success has obviously made my life very comfortable, but I honestly couldn't care less about making piles more, although I know a lot of people don't believe me when I say this. I've experienced life on both sides of the track, and I discovered at a very early age just how hard some people have to work for their daily bread and how awful some jobs can be. Because I've been there, I don't feel distanced or different from people who are doing that now. Once, for example, when we were having a discussion about our crew and how we should treat them, I remember getting a bit heated and saying to David, 'You've never worked in anything but the rarefied world of music, have you?' 'No,' he admitted. My experience, though, was very different, and so I never feel that I am the artist, they are the workmen and therefore we are on different social levels. In fact, sometimes, when I find myself on stage, having to be charming and looking pretty when I don't feel like it, I think I'd rather be loading trucks.

Recordings are challenging, videos and promotion are necessary, but singing live in front of a big audience is certainly what makes our hearts beat faster.

So far, the most significant and satisfying moment for me to do with money occurred some years ago, when my mother was experiencing a low period and was scared about what the future held for her. Even though I didn't live in Switzerland anymore, I happened to be home at that time. I put an arm around her shoulder and said, 'Don't worry, Mum, I will always take care of you.' It was just wonderful to see her insecurity dissolve and appreciate just how incredibly happy I had made her feel. She almost started crying. Before then, I think she was always afraid that there would be no one to care for her when she could no longer do it for herself. My mother had to take care of five children on one salary and it is thanks to her that we have grown up to be the people we are, with such good sense when it comes to money. She brought her children up to be independent and sometimes, I think she fears, a bit *too* independent. But the basic family bond has always been there, and always will be. Family is family forever.

What I would really love to do some time in the near future is take my family on one of our Il Divo trips, so they can get the chance to fly around in a private jet, be picked up by limousines and sleep in five-star hotel suites. I really will try to organize that, although it won't be easy as they all work so hard.

As for me, I've seen and done a lot in the last three years. The first stretch-limousine ride is really cool, but then you discover that they are actually not that comfortable. These days, I don't care if I sit in the luggage van, as long as it gets me to the airport. I do enjoy the luxury of a five-star suite. It's great staying in nice hotels and having breakfast in your room and having someone to tidy up after you. And the fact that we don't have to worry about day-to-day things, such as buying food or paying bills, is very comfortable. At the same time I'm aware that I am paying for all this luxury out of my own pocket. But our lifestyle does involve sacrifices, so we indulge ourselves where we can.

As for me, I've now seen and done a lot. The first stretch-limousine ride is really cool, but then you discover that they are actually not that comfortable.

I also love that being part of Il Divo has allowed me to meet so many interesting, powerful people. I can hardly believe that I have met Bill Clinton, George Bush and Mikhail Gorbachev, within two months last winter. When we met President Bush at Christmas in Washington, I remember saying to the other guys, 'No matter what anybody thinks about this man's policies, meeting him was impressive.' He came across as a really genuine guy, and standing on the stage singing, with him in the middle of the first row smiling and nodding his approval was quite extraordinary. 'The President of the United States of America has just shown his appreciation for what I am doing,' I thought. 'That's really quite something.'

Mikhail Gorbachev came across as such a warm, passionate person. He took my hand in both of his and held it, Russian style, for at least a minute while telling me how much he liked our performance. We only met the Clintons very briefly, backstage for a picture at a Barbra Streisand show in Madison Square Garden, New York. Hillary said she was a big fan of ours and had all our albums.

Political leaders aside, there are lots of musicians I admire who I would love to meet. First of all the great tenors: Pavarotti, Domingo and Carreras; then my guitar heroes: George Lynch, Yngwie J. Malmsteen and Eddie van Halen. These are all people I would like to sit down and have a real conversation with, and maybe even a lesson or two.

Before the tour with Barbra, we had never shared the stage with somebody who'd achieved such a legendary status. It's something that we will always remember. She is the consummate professional; there are no singers of her calibre anymore. It was such a joy to work alongside her, not only to sing with her, but to watch how she commands the audience. She holds them in the palm of her hand, draws them in completely and somehow manages to make 20,000 people feel like each one is sitting at home with her. There are moments when the audience is so focused you could hear a pin drop.

Barbra has always had a huge gay following and since appearing with her, interviewers have often said to us, 'Are you aware that Il Divo now has many gay fans?'

Once, at a concert we did in San Francisco, there was a gay couple in the third row and when we sang 'All By Myself', one of the guys burst into tears. I found that very endearing. To me there's no difference – him or her, straight or gay, as long as they're being moved by the music.

Although we loved being on stage with Barbra for two months, there is absolutely nothing that compares with being on our own tours and performing our own, almost two-hour-long show. That is just so special. Our most recent world tour included Southeast Asia, South America, Australia, Canada, South Africa and Europe, so it was an incredibly busy time for us.

Our arrival in Japan was particularly exciting, absolutely fantastic. There were literally hundreds of people waiting for us at the airport, something that had never happened before, and, for the first time in my life, I felt like a superstar.

As the Japanese security staff rushed forward, I got a hint of what it must have been like to be one of the Beatles, who were greeted like that wherever they went. For safety reasons, the security staff tried to rush us through the mass of screaming Japanese women, but it was not an easy task. There were several moments when we were nearly stopped in our tracks by the sheer enthusiasm of the crowd. We adore our fans, but when there are so many trying to get close to us at the same time, I must admit, it is quite scary. Later on in that world tour, the same kind of welcome was in store for us when we arrived in South America.

Once you are well known, security guards are absolutely essential. You can't even make it across the street without them. It's not so much your security that's at stake, it's your freedom to move around, to get from A to B. As much as we enjoy the attention, you do get tired of all the hassle sometimes, especially when we are jet-lagged.

I would have loved to have seen more of Japan and the Japanese people, but sightseeing isn't really possible on tours, there simply is no time for it. In fact, it was impossible for us to leave our hotel rooms without having our pictures taken or being asked for autographs. Doing the shows, though, was amazing, and the audience's response continued to be overwhelming throughout.

I was very impressed by the Japanese people. For instance, when we went on the train from Tokyo to Osaka and then back to Tokyo three days later, I absentmindedly left my iPod on the seat. When I told our Japanese tour manager what I had done, he immediately leapt into action. He phoned the train company and was told that my iPod had been handed into the lost property office and was waiting there for collection. I thought that was very telling about the Japanese people. I have had so many things disappear on our travels that I never expected to see it again.

Sometimes, I feel my life is on hold. I love what I am doing now and I want it to continue for as long as I still enjoy it, but one day I will go back to living a life that belongs to me.

These days, we just never stop working. After touring the whole of South America, we had just two days off in Toronto before we began the Canadian leg of the tour. Even when we have time off, it doesn't feel like a proper break, because we are always gearing up for the next lap. Likewise, we don't really have weekends. There's no rhythm or structure to our work. When we are on a tour, it's basically show, travel, show, travel. We completely lose track of the time and what day of the week it is. It might seem like a glamorous life staying in luxurious hotels all the time, but we are never in our own space and so we can never fully relax as we would at home.

Sometimes, I feel my life is on hold. I love what I am doing now and I want it to continue for as long as I still enjoy it, but one day I will go back to living a life that belongs to me.

And when that time comes I'll buy myself a big, old motorbike, leap aboard and hit the road. The only difference this time will be the very special passenger riding on the back, and when I feel her arms around me, I'll say to myself, 'What's the hurry? I think I'll ride on for a while before I start looking for another job.'

Simon Cowell

I had a vision with Il Divo to find four of the most talented undiscovered classical singers and attempt to turn this group into the biggest-selling act in the world. I had no idea how difficult this would be. We auditioned hundreds of singers all over the world and only four impressed us – Carlos, David, Sébastien and Urs. Not only did these guys have incredible voices, they had charm, charisma and ambition.

The four guys knew what type of record they wanted to make and their success has been astonishing. In three years they have sold over 18 million records and have changed the public's perception of opera forever.

Success can breed monsters but not these guys. They have remained polite and charming and I am proud to have been a part of their phenomenal success.

Dainty Consolidated Entertainment Presents
IL DIVO
LIVE
VODAFONE ARENA FRIDAY 16 FEB
ON SALE MONDAY 13 NOV
BOOK AT
TICKETEK 132 849 OR TICKETEK.COM

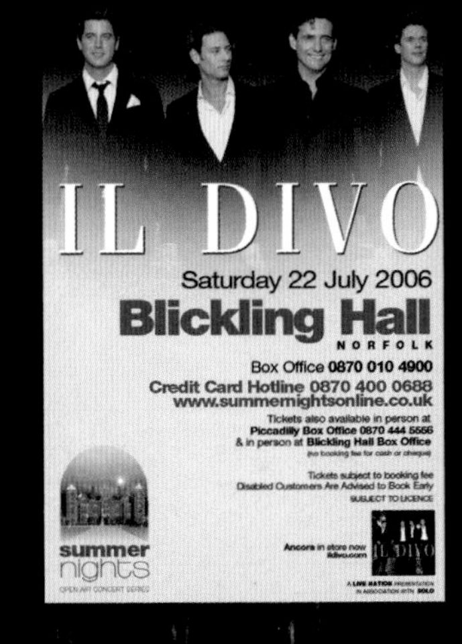
IL DIVO
Saturday 22 July 2006
Blickling Hall
NORFOLK
Box Office 0870 010 4900
Credit Card Hotline 0870 400 0688
www.summernightsonline.co.uk
Tickets also available in person at
Piccadilly Box Office 0870 444 5556
& in person at Blickling Hall Box Office
Tickets subject to booking fee
Disabled Customers Are Advised to Book Early
SUBJECT TO LICENCE
summer
nights

IL DIVO
IN CONCERT
SPECIAL GUEST
KATIE MELUA
JULY 3
GENERAL MOTORS PLACE

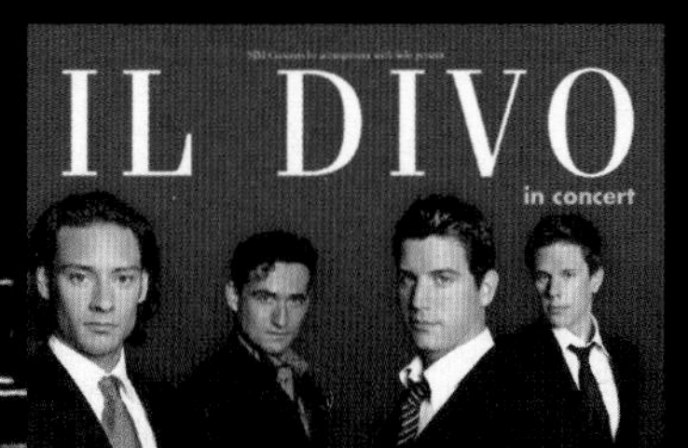
IL DIVO
in concert
with special guest
Hayley Westenra
MARCH 2006
Wed 29th Cardiff International Arena SOLD OUT
Thu 30th Brighton Centre SOLD OUT
APRIL 2006
Sat 1st Nottingham Arena SOLD OUT
Sun 2nd Birmingham NEC SOLD OUT
Tue 4th Newcastle Metro Radio Arena SOLD OUT
Thu 6th Glasgow SOLD OUT
Fri 7th Clyde Auditorium SOLD OUT
Sun 9th Manchester Evening News Arena SOLD OUT
Tue 11th London SOLD OUT
Wed 12th Wembley Arena SOLD OUT

STREISAND
IL DIVO
GARDEN
American Express
ALL TICKETS AVAILABLE THROUGH

IL DIVO LIVE
WORLD TOUR 2007

'FALL IN LOVE WITH MUSIC AGAIN'
IL DIVO
WEMBLEY ARENA
16 MAY 2007
THE NEW ALBUM
SIEMPRE
OUT NOW!